GW00492679

CHIEFS OF STAFF

THE PORTRAIT COLLECTION OF THE IRISH DEFENCE FORCES

EDITED BY

COLONEL TOM HODSON (RETD)

The History Press Ireland

First published 2011

The History Press Ireland
119 Lower Baggot Street
Dublin 2
Ireland
www.thehistorypress.ie

Essays © the contributors, 2011
Images © the artists and their estates, 2011

The right of Tom Hodson to be identified as the Editor
of this work has been asserted in accordance with the
Copyrights, Designs and Patents Act 1988.

All rights reserved. No part of this book may be reprinted
or reproduced or utilised in any form or by any electronic,
mechanical or other means, now known or hereafter invented,
including photocopying and recording, or in any information
storage or retrieval system, without the permission in writing
from the Publishers.

British Library Cataloguing in Publication Data.
A catalogue record for this book is available from the British Library.

ISBN 978 1 84588 991 3

Typesetting and origination by The History Press

CONTENTS

Mary McAleese

FOREWORD

Uachtarán na hÉireann
President of Ireland

Message from President McAleese

It gives me great pleasure to congratulate McKee Officers' Club on the publication of this remarkable book celebrating this unique and historic art collection.

Visitors to McKee Officers' Mess, who have seen its portraits of the Chiefs of Staff of the Defence Forces, are undoubtedly impressed by this portrait collection. Only its location, rightfully at the heart of the McKee Officers' Mess, precludes it from a wider exposure and so I am particularly pleased that the McKee Officers Club has undertaken the task of introducing the collection to a more general audience.

However, there is more to this book than exposure and publicity. The portrait collection is a unique, historic and complete pictorial record of the Chiefs of Staff of the Defence Forces, from General Michael Collins to the late Lieutenant General Dermot Earley. This book records, analyses and above all celebrates the far-sighted decision taken more than sixty years ago by the members of the Mess which led to the creation and the continuation of this important contribution to the patrimony, not only of the Defence Forces, but also of the nation.

The founders of the collection and their successors over the years were concerned not only with recording their commanders, but also with having them recorded by the foremost Irish portrait painters of the time. They have been successful in this concern, as can be seen in the illustrious names, past and present, to be found in the book.

The various contributions to the book bring to light the history and the importance of the collection, and also its wider significance to art history and to the history of the Defence Forces. As the supreme command of the Defence Forces is vested by Bunreacht na hÉireann in the President, I am happy to note the possibility that the inspiration for the collection may have been given by our first President Douglas Hyde, with the gift of his portrait to the Army in 1944, which now hangs facing that of General Michael Collins.

I thank all those who have been involved in the establishment, conservation and promotion of this collection from its inauguration to the present day. Your generosity and efforts have created and nurtured this unique collection which has not merely huge historical interest but also great artistic merit. I also congratulate all those involved in the detailed research and preparation that went into this book and I hope that its many readers will enjoy this new overview of this wonderful collection.

Mary McAleese

MARY MCALEESE
PRESIDENT OF IRELAND
10 February 2011

ACKNOWLEDGEMENTS

McKee Officers Club has been extremely fortunate, and is deeply appreciative of the support it has received during this project, beginning of course with being honoured by President Mary McAleese's gracious agreement to contribute the foreword to the book. The Minister for Defence has been supportive, and the Chief of Staff, Lieutenant General Sean McCann and his Deputy Chief of Staff (Support), Major General Dave Ashe have been unflagging in their co-operation and assistance. The Officer Commanding the Mess and also the Mess President, Commandant Pauline O'Connell, have at all times assisted the club with facilities and research.

The book has been greatly enhanced by our contributors: Mr James Hanley RHA; Colonel Tom Hodson (Retd), who also edited; Mr Donal Maguire, National Gallery of Ireland; Lieutenant General Colm Mangan DSM (Retd); Dr Pat Murphy HRHA, and Professor Eunan O'Halpin. Others have also been generous with their help, including Commandant Victor Laing and all of his staff in Military Archives, Colonel William Nott (Retd) and Commandant Billy Campbell (Retd). Dr Brendan Rooney of the NGI was an early and enthusiastic friend of the project, and Ann Hodge, Curator of Prints and Drawings at the NGI, also kindly contributed.

Thanks are due to all of the artists or their estates for permission to reproduce the portraits. Ms Louise Morgan of NGI and Ms Elizabeth Igoe of IVARO helped enormously in this important process. In spite of extensive enquiries, it was not possible to establish copyright approval for the portraits by Richard A. Free, and for this we apologise. Ms Sarah Le Jeune was extremely helpful with information on her father James Le Jeune RHA, as indeed was Ms Rosita Boland on her uncle Gerald Bruen RHA. The President of the RHA kindly permitted reproduction of the career details of their past president, Dr Tom Ryan. Dr Ryan himself has been very generous with details on his own works and with other information on the collection. Mr Donard de Cogan very kindly gave access to his extensive archive on his late father, Commandant Maurice F. Cogan.

We have been very fortunate with our publishers, The History Press Ireland. Mr Ronan Colgan and his colleagues have been responsible for the excellent design, printing and production of the work. A work of this type would not be possible without a high standard of photography and in this all our expectations have been surpassed by Commandant Paddy Walshe (Retd) and his outstanding team at Photo Processing.

We hope that this book is a fitting tribute to the former Chiefs of Staff, the artists who painted their portraits, the committees and, most importantly, the mess members of McKee Officers' Mess.

Colonel Joseph O'Sullivan (Retd), President McKee Officers' Club Council

ESTABLISHING AND MAINTAINING THE COLLECTION

MILITARY READERS may recognise in the title of this essay an oblique reference to the tactical requirement to 'Gain and maintain contact with the enemy'. While it is true that the Chiefs of Staff Portrait Collection in McKee Officers' Mess is somewhat ironically known to mess members as 'the rogues gallery', it is not at all the intention to imply any feelings of enmity between the members and the collection or indeed the sitters. On the contrary, it is my aim to show the affection which the members have had for the collection for more than sixty years. This affection, and indeed respect, will I hope become apparent in the recounting of the vision shown in the creation of the collection, the steadfastness shown in its continuation and the recent generosity of the members in funding its conservation. This generosity has of course been matched in recent years by the generosity of the State through successive Ministers for Defence.

It is tempting to identify the genesis of the collection in President Douglas Hyde's gift of his fine portrait to the Army in October 1944. This portrait by Sean O'Sullivan RHA graces, and indeed dominates, the view of those entering the mess dining room, where it is a magnificent foil to the portrait of General Michael Collins.[1] President Hyde's engaging, informal portrait, with the half-smoked cigarette, harks back to an earlier age, and the commemorative plaque proclaiming, 'É féin do bhron ar an airm', may well have revealed the possibilities of the room for a portrait collection. If indeed so, it was to be another seven years before such a collection materialised. In the meantime, as Dr J. Patrick Murphy so excellently narrates in a subsequent essay, the president's gift had other, more immediate, and more eminent consequences.

While many soldiers will have recognised the military reference in the title, the more civilised majority of readers may not be aware that the mess is the one area in a soldier's life where he or she can expect to be dealt with somewhat democratically. According to Defence Forces Regulations, 'each officer will be a member of the Officers' Mess of the unit or barracks on the strength of which he is borne or to which he is attached for any period in excess of 30 days'.[2] The mess, which provides accommodation, dining and recreational facilities, is managed by a Mess Committee elected by all the members of the mess. This committee takes direction from the members at regular mess meetings, where matters are voted on and decided by a majority of members.

Being a military establishment, however, the democratic nature of this arrangement is to some extent modified by the fact that the senior officer of the unit is nominated by regulations as the Officer Commanding the Mess. While he may not interfere in voting at mess meetings, the Officer Commanding the Mess can have an important function in the correct running of the mess to the benefit of all officers. In the case of McKee Barracks Officers' Mess, which is the mess of Defence Forces Headquarters, the Officer Commanding the Mess was either the Chief of Staff or was nominated by him. This provision was of crucial importance for the establishment of the Chiefs of Staff Portrait Collection, for on 13 June 1950, the then Chief of Staff, Major General Liam Archer, presiding over a mess meeting, indicated his support for a proposal by Commandant Moran, seconded by Captain Jim Millar, 'That representations of Commanders-in-Chief and Chiefs of Staff be hung in the mess and that where such could not be obtained plaques should be put in their allocated place.'[3] Major General Archer supported the proposal, although aware of the potential difficulties and costs to the mess. His support was vital, because at the same meeting, the members had agreed to provide £150 to £200 for a bust of Dick McKee, after whom the mess was named, and also to pay for two tons of coal per month, from September to April, to provide heating for the ground floor of the mess and for dishwashing.

A special committee, headed by Colonel James Flynn, Assistant Chief of Staff, and comprising Commandant Harrington and Captains Cogan and Millar, was tasked to investigate and report back to the members. While this is the first official mention in mess minutes, the files also include a memo drawn up by Colonel Flynn in February 1950. The memo suggests that a proposal to provide paintings 'of a distinctly national military interest and if possible of such a nature that the collection may be added to over the years' be put to a mess meeting. It seems that, as is often the case, the ground was being prepared beforehand.

Colonel Flynn's committee reported back to an extraordinary general meeting two months later, with precise recommendations that the first three portraits be commissioned from two prominent Irish portrait painters of the time, Leo Whelan and Margaret Clarke. Without encroaching on the expertise of other contributors, it is clear that a statement of intent and excellence was being made by the committee. Its choice of subjects was not, however, without some opposition, with one member proposing that Patrick Pearse should be included as the first Commander-in-Chief of the Army. The Chief of Staff recognised the difficulty surrounding the discussion, and when it was proposed that 'the Chiefs of Staff of the other side should not be omitted from the collection of pictures', Major General Archer ruled the subject out of order and he trusted that the proposer 'would understand that he could not allow discussion on the matter'.

The committee's funding proposals proved less contentious, and the members voted that a sum of £130 be added to an existing special fund of £515 in order to proceed with the initial and subsequent portraits. It would seem that the chosen artists viewed their commissions as being more than mere commercial enterprises, as the committee's briefing recorded that, 'the special rates quoted by the artists concerned are much below the prices normally received by them, and it is requested that the cost be treated as confidential'. Other important aspects of the collection were laid down at this meeting. A standard size of 30" x 25" was adopted, with the exception of the Collins portrait, which was a replica of one hanging in Dáil Éireann, and one which the artist felt would be ruined if reduced.

The dining room was adopted as the preferred location for the portraits on the recommendation of Mr Thomas McGreevy, then Director of the National Gallery of Ireland, who also advised against mixing paintings and photographs. It was accepted by the members that the collection should be of paintings only; a prescient decision, as was to be shown some fifty years later. The special committee was requested to continue its work, and when it was reported at the Quarterly General Mess Meeting held some sixty years ago, on 24 April 1951, that the portraits of Generals Collins, Mulcahy and McMahon had been completed and delivered, the Chiefs of Staff Portrait Collection at McKee Barracks Officers' Mess was effectively established. Colonel Flynn informed the meeting that while seven more portraits were required to complete the collection, his subcommittee was confident that if the members were to vote another £300 they should be able to provide another three portraits in the following twelve months. He expressed their intention to commission different artists, 'so as to make the collection more interesting', a concern which was to occupy future subcommittees. The Chief of Staff enthusiastically supported the proposal on the basis that 'the collection would be of great value and interest in the future'.

Major General Archer was not only instrumental in establishing the collection; it must be acknowledged that his influence was essential. The financial outlay was considerable and may not have been voted for by the mess members but for his vision and leadership. Indeed, following his retirement, the pace slackened somewhat, with four more portraits being commissioned between 1951 and 1956, when the then Chief of Staff, Major General Patrick Mulcahy, proposed the re-establishment of a portraits subcommittee, which was renamed the Portraits Committee. This was accepted, along with the added proposal that £10 per month should be set aside with the aim of providing at least one portrait each year. At this stage there were five portraits outstanding.

The committee was re-established, with several of the earlier members, but the financial situation was apparently unfavourable, as at a meeting one year later, the members were informed that it had not been possible to set aside the previously agreed £10. It was a critical moment, but the mess members adopted the radical option of increasing the general fund by 1s per member per month. While the sum might today seem derisory, it was radical then, as Defence Forces Regulations prohibit the levying of subscriptions other than for the general and messing funds 'against mess members without a majority vote of the general body of members and the sanction of the Officer Commanding the Mess'.[4] The earlier vision prevailed, and avoided the need, in what were difficult financial times, of generating a majority vote in favour of continuing the collection.

Three further portraits were commissioned between 1957 and 1960. It is interesting to note the punctiliousness of the committee, who agreed that a commission be given to one of its members, Captain M.F. Cogan, to paint the portrait of Major General Joseph Sweeney. Captain Cogan requested that he be allowed resign from the committee, but its chairman, Colonel Flynn, said that this was not possible, as he had been elected by the general body of the mess members. It was, however, 'permissible for Captain Cogan to absent himself from Committee meetings until the commission had been executed'. Captain Cogan was obviously aware of the financial difficulties faced by the committee, as his generous offer to paint the portrait for 50 guineas was accepted. It is also gratifying to note that, in spite of there being only £91 available to the Portraits Committee, the Mess President informed a mess meeting on 5 December 1960 that 'arrangements were finalised for the painting of a portrait of Lieutenant General Archer'. The two outstanding portraits were provided, so in 1971, following the long tenure of Lieutenant General Sean McKeown DSM as Chief of Staff, the collection was complete, with the one exception being that of Major General Sean Collins-Powell who served as Chief of Staff while Lieutenant General McKeown DSM served as Force Commander ONUC. It would not have been appropriate to commission Major General Sean Collins-Powell's portrait earlier, as he did not retire from the Defence Forces until January 1969.

Unfortunately, that number increased to three in 1971 with the retirement of Lieutenant General McKeown DSM and the untimely death in service of Major General Patrick Delaney. The incoming Chief of Staff, Major General Thomas Leslie O'Carroll, was briefed on the affairs of the mess and the status of the portrait collection, including the sum of £52 remaining for commissions. As before, a Portrait Committee was established, which, with the financial support of the members, commissioned portraits of Lieutenant General McKeown DSM and Major General Collins-Powell. The case of Major General Delaney's portrait is instructive insofar as it retained the original intention of the collection's founders. An initial portrait of the general in United Nations fatigues was accepted by the mess until a portrait in keeping with the formal portraits of other Chiefs of Staff was commissioned. This was finally achieved in 1984.

In his report to the Chief of Staff, Lieutenant Colonel Gerard V. Coghlan, successor to Colonel Flynn as Chairman of the Portrait Committee, referred to the continuing difficulty of sourcing frames for the portraits. He reported that 'the search for suitable frames has been put in hand. You will probably be aware that the usual, indeed the only source is the purchase of old pictures in the city auction rooms, the [useless] pictures being discarded.' Fortunately, this unsatisfactory situation no longer applies, as commissions now include the requirement that the artist supplies the frame.

The 1980s also saw a change in the tempo and pattern of commissions and acquisitions. Major General O'Carroll's portrait was acquired in 1983, albeit some seven years after he retired, but from then on, the practice of arranging the Chief of Staff's portrait, either before or just after he retired, was established. The Portrait Committee concept was not, however, allowed lapse, as a committee was formed to advise on the artist and cost for each subsequent portrait. The Mess Committee also recognised the need not only to continue the collection, but to maintain it, and provided funding for the cleaning of the portraits and for having glass fitted to each of them. Their foresight was to prove helpful to their successors, more than twenty years later.

While the 1980s may have seen certain regularity in the life of the collection, its future was by no means assured, as the cost of commissioning portraits appropriate to the vision of its founders was increasing substantially. By 1998, the cost of commissioning a formal portrait of the retiring Chief of Staff had risen to €6,000. That this was a substantial sum to demand of the mess members every few years was recognised by the Minister for Defence, who agreed to provide a substantial grant. Other Defence Forces messes contributed to the cost, with the bulk of the remainder being voted to the Mess Committee by the members. This period also saw a situation in which one retiring Chief of Staff, Lieutenant General David Stapleton DSM, who was acutely aware of the cost implications, decided that the medium for his portrait should be a specially commissioned photograph. While the photograph was of a particularly high quality, it was not in keeping with the collection, and ran the risk of diminishing its status. The photograph was replaced in 2008 with a fine portrait by James Hanley RHA.

The generosity of the State has continued, with subsequent portraits being provided for from the Defence Forces budget allocation. However, the mess members were not absolved of the responsibility for the collection, and their generosity was again tested in 2007, when the Mess President presented a proposal to an extraordinary general mess meeting that a sum of €50,000 be voted for the restoration and conservation of the portraits and frames. The meeting was extraordinary and so was the proposal. The members were advised of the urgent necessity for the project and that it would be inappropriate to seek State funding for the preservation of mess assets. Despite the substantial cost involved, the members were not found wanting and voted an initial grant of €20,000, to be followed by later grants in 2008 and 2009. The project was in fact completed in 2008 at a total cost, from members' contributions, of €40,000.

It is perhaps appropriate that this short account of the collection's life should close with recognition of the continuing exceptional generosity of the mess members. They have shown themselves loyal to the vision and courage of their predecessors in cherishing and continuing their valuable patrimony. The latest addition to the collection, the portrait of the much respected, admired and indeed greatly missed leader Lieutenant General Dermot Earley DSM has taken its allotted place in the ranks, to the right of General Michael Collins. It is to be hoped, however, that it will be a temporary place and that in keeping with the tradition of the collection and of the mess, it will in turn take one pace to the right and be replaced with the portraits of future Chiefs of Staff.

Colonel Tom Hodson (Retd), BA (Mod), MLitt

OUR COMMANDERS-IN-CHIEF
AND CHIEFS OF STAFF

BUILT BY the British in 1888, McKee Barracks survives as an interesting example of late nineteenth-century architecture in Ireland. A fascinating complex of buildings, it remains an important feature of the architectural fabric of Dublin city today. Since 1922 it has been occupied by the Irish Defence Forces, and the barracks has established a strong social and cultural presence within the northern inner city. Within the sporting community, it is well known as the home of the Irish Army's Equitation School, and Army riders from McKee have represented Ireland in show-jumping competitions at Olympic, World and European Championship level. However, despite such cultural acclaim, neither McKee Barracks nor the Irish Army has been recognised for contributing to Ireland's visual cultural heritage. Yet, unbeknown to many, the Barracks is home to the nation's only collection of portraits of Ireland's Commanders-in-Chief and Chiefs of Staff.

The collection hangs principally on the walls above the dining tables of the Officers' Mess and extends out along the adjacent corridor. Comprising twenty-eight pictures in all, the portraits both document and honour the individuals who have occupied the most senior position within Ireland's Defence Forces. Ireland's Chief of Staff is responsible for the overall control of the Irish Army, Naval Service, Air Corps and Reserve Defence Force. Beginning with a portrait of Michael Collins, this visual record currently concludes with an image of Lieutenant General Dermot Earley DSM, who retired in 2010.

The portrait of Collins takes prime position above the dining room's fireplace, its prominence reflecting the sitter's immense status and influence in the history of the organisation. To Collins's left, in accordance with tradition, hangs the portrait of the most recently retired Chief of Staff. Next to this, the portrait of his predecessor is, in turn, followed by his and so continues, in reverse chronological order, the arrangement of the collection. Presented in this fashion, the portraits evoke a strong sense of the history and lineage associated with this branch of Irish culture. Indeed, sitting in the wood-panelled mess hall, surrounded by the portraits of these influential and commanding figures, one has the uncanny feeling of being in their company, their ubiquitous spirits still overseeing the day-to-day activities of the barracks.

It is the capacity to capture a likeness and evoke the presence of a person in this way that makes portraiture such a powerful and fascinating form of representation. Portraits are intrinsically linked with the unique identity of the pictured individual, a relationship that distinguishes the genre from all other forms of representational art. Thomas Bodkin, former Director of the National Gallery of Ireland, recognised this when he observed that, 'people who value character more than imagination will always be prone to indulge a strong predilection for the art of portraiture'.[5] Portraits are most obviously associated with the description of a person's physical features, yet this simple understanding belies the achievements of the genre. Portraits have the capacity to reveal complex qualities of character, such as age, gender, social status, profession, and even aspects of a sitter's relationship with others. Such abstract characteristics are changeable but generally expressive of the expectations and circumstances of a particular time and society. In 1909, the Austrian critic Hans Tietze argued that the portrait, 'cannot be detached from more general stylistic events … The portraitist is … forced into a compromise between his own personal perception of the subject and conventions which may be of a more outward or more inward nature.'[6]

There is a duality to portraiture based on the tension between the perception of individual likeness and generic type. The portrait is both a symbolic and iconographic image that exploits recognised social and visual codes that are easily interpreted by the viewer. Indeed, before the advent of photography, the portrayal of a sitter's generic or conventional qualities was prioritised over the representation of their more unique attributes. In eighteenth- and early nineteenth-century political and professional portraits, it was more important to document a sitter's occupation and social position than their individual character. In works such as Anthony Lee's portrait of Joseph Leeson at the National Gallery of Ireland, for example, specific gestures, clothing, accessories and postures were used to provide clues to the sitter's public identity, the nature of their profession or their gentlemanly interests. In some cases, an accurate description of a sitter's appearance was of little consequence at all to the successful portrayal of the subject.

The portrait collection in McKee Barracks represents twenty-eight very different individuals, yet, rather than focusing on the diverse qualities of each sitter, precedence is given to the single shared aspect of their identity. The sitters are primarily defined by their professional role as Commander-in-Chief or Chief of Staff of the Defence Forces. This rank is most obviously conveyed in the accurate description of the General, Lieutenant or Major General's uniform, identified by the rank markings displayed on the collar and the shoulder epaulettes. Interestingly, the evolution of the design of the uniform can be traced across the portrait series. The original, as seen in Collins's portrait, was adapted from the uniform worn by the Irish Volunteers and featured a high-collared jacket. This was later replaced by a lapel, as first seen in the portrait of Major General Liam Egan. Out of sync with the other sitters, Major General Michael Brennan and Major General Thomas Leslie O'Carroll are portrayed in the more formal and visually striking officer's dress uniform. The various accoutrements associated with the position are also included in many of the portraits. The cap, gloves and Sam Browne belt are distinguishing elements of a commissioned officer's uniform and are exploited for their symbolic qualities. Although the gloves only feature in nine of the portraits, the cap, which prominently displays the badge of the Chief of Staff, is worn or held under the arm of a number of the sitters. By emphasising the generic and emblematic qualities of their identity in this way, each figure is presented as a character type, one that can be identified by the viewer and understood within this particular social context.

It is debatable whether a portrait can ever provide a truly authentic interpretation of an individual identity – a dilemma that Thomas Bodkin found particularly problematic when choosing definitive likenesses for the portrait collection at the National Gallery of Ireland. In his 1936 essay 'Some Problems of National Portraiture', Bodkin addressed the issue by drawing attention to a selection of four likenesses of MP John Philpot Curran, which date from between 1798 and 1807, by four different artists: Hugh Douglas Hamilton, Thomas Lawrence, James Petrie and an unidentified artist. Each artist took a distinctly different approach to interpreting the sitter. Bodkin notes that the portraits exemplify 'the profound differences which can exist between authentic likenesses of the same individual'.[7] Bodkin's argument alludes to the difficulties associated with the representation of character and personality and how this affects the portrayal and perception of likeness. The evocation of intangible characteristics, or what is often referred to as an individual's soul or inner being, became particularly apparent in portraits from the mid-nineteenth century onwards. Following the advent of commercial photography, the expression and interpretation of an individual's 'inner being' was vital to the continued relevance of the genre. A sitter's internal qualities are not simply reproduced, but rather mediated through the mind and hand of the artist through the subtle employment of signs and visual messages. Such subtleties are subject to the prevailing aesthetic judgements of a society, as well as the viewer's own unique expectations. As a result, any interpretation of individual character or personality is highly subjective.

For many modern portraitists, such as those who contributed to this collection, capturing the essence of an individual's character relies on a process of interaction between the artist and the sitter. This is traditionally carried out at a portrait sitting, during which artists often develop a rapport with their sitter while taking photographs or making multiple sketches in an attempt to construct different elements of mood and character. How the artist sees the subject during these sittings is as important as how the sitter wishes to be seen. The philosopher Hans-Georg Gadamer referred to this phenomenon as 'occasionality', in which the portrait's allusion to the sitter is a product of the artist's intention.[8] The term draws attention to the creative act and how it is fundamental to the production of a likeness. This significant aspect of the genre reveals how a portrait is defined not only by its connection to a sitter but also by the series of decisions and negotiations associated with the more complex interrelationship of the sitter, the artist and the viewer.

The collection at McKee Barracks offers the viewer an interesting dynamic in this respect. While most of the portraits were painted from life and involved a sitting, nine, from Collins to Michael Brennan, were painted retrospectively or posthumously and most likely after photographs. Such a discrepancy could potentially undermine the authenticity of the portrait image, but it was an unavoidable consequence of the portrait series having been initiated in 1950. The first portrait to be commissioned was that of Lieutenant General Peadar McMahon by Maurice McGonigal. McMahon was Chief of Staff from 1924 to 1927, after which he was appointed Secretary of the Department of Defence, a position he held until 1958. He retired as Chief of Staff at the age of forty-four, yet the portrait depicts a man of approximately sixty-eight, suggesting that it was painted from life. This was followed seven years later by an image of one of McMahon's successors, Lieutenant General Michael Brennan, by Seán Keating. To the detriment of the portrait, it seems Keating relied on photographic sources in his production of a likeness. The sitter's absence from the portrait transaction is palpable, as the image lacks the vitality and presence of character that is discernible in MacGonigal's work. This was noted by the Chairman of the Chief of Staff Portrait Committee, who was pleased with Keating's 'excellent and detailed treatment of the dress uniform', but conveyed the 'disagreement amongst [the committee] to the closeness of likeness to the man himself'.[9] The chairman's comments highlight a significant crux in portraiture's relationship with identity; likeness is ultimately formed in the mind of the viewer, who will always respond to what they know of the person as much as the visual information provided.[10]

The difficulties associated with communicating character and personality in a portrait derived from a photograph are further evidenced in the images of Lieutenant General Daniel Hogan by George Collie and Lieutenant General Sean McKeown DSM by Maurice F. Cogan. Collie was an accomplished academic painter who trained under William Orpen and Seán Keating at the Metropolitan School of Art. However, though the figure of Hogan is confidently and accurately modelled, there seems to be an indifference in the representation of character that is also evident in the portrait of McKeown. These images seem to do little more than mimic the type of formal photograph from which they are most likely reproduced. In contrast, in the portraits of General Richard Mulcahy and General Sean McMahon, the artists Leo Whelan and Margaret Clarke took a more subjective approach in handling the portrayal of character. While the likenesses are also most likely adapted from photographs, the images have been greatly enhanced by a creative and eloquent construction of mood and atmosphere in the paintings. The dramatic use of light and shade in particular lends the compositions a striking and theatrical effect that is missing from the other portraits. The figures in both portraits are depicted seated in darkened interiors and there is a deliberate sense of poise and equanimity in their portrayal. Mulcahy is captured in a moment of thought, pausing from the work that is laid out on his desk, while McMahon's relaxed pose contrasts with his intense gaze, which appears to pierce the very picture plane. The paintings draw on the viewer's imagination and various aspects of the sitters' public identities to bestow upon the subjects a more authentic sense of individual character. In the absence of a sitter's direct involvement, these visual conceits provide a narrative counter-point to which the viewer can emotionally respond. Both sitters played pivotal roles in the formation of the Irish Free State and their identities, in many ways, have become intertwined with the dramatic events of that historic period. The portraits personify, in the mind of the viewer, their passion and idealism, along with many of the other self-sacrificing qualities associated with those people who contributed to the foundation of the State.

This form of artistic invention is perhaps most effectively realised in Leo Whelan's posthumous and iconic portrayal of Michael Collins. The portrait focuses on the subject's celebrated reputation as a heroic and inspirational leader, and depicts Collins standing proudly against the Irish landscape. However, the likeness and pose was copied from a well-known black and white photograph, taken at the funeral of Arthur Griffith on 12 August 1922. The original photograph shows Collins surrounded by military personnel and catches him as he glances across the crowd, perhaps at something that has captured his attention. It is one of the last known photographs of Collins, who was killed only ten days later, during an ambush at Béal na mBláth in County Cork. For the retrospective viewer, and indeed the painter, an awareness of the imminent fate that awaits the young man adds a deep sense of poignancy to the photograph. However, in his painting, Whelan has vanquished the tragic connotations of the image by transforming it into a celebration of the subject's life and legacy. Collins is removed from the crowded photograph and singled out for individual attention. He stands erect, dressed in full uniform. His uneasy glance across the crowd has been replaced by a confident and purposeful gaze over the Irish landscape. The motif is a reminder to the viewer that it is this land to which the subject belongs and for which he has fought and ultimately given his life. Collins is the only figure in the collection of the Chief of Staff portraits to be shown wearing his officer's gloves. Clasping his hands with purpose, the accessory is used as a means of communicating character, and signifies that, above all, Collins was a man of action. Rather than engaging the viewer, he appears to be contemplating the battlefield, perhaps deliberating on his next move. This suggestion of impending conflict is further implied in the gloomy and tempestuous clouds that have gathered in the sky above Collins's head.

While some of the portraits, particularly the more recent works, incorporate neutral backdrops, many exploit background detail for symbolic effect or as a means of communicating information relating to aspects of the sitter's identity. Landscape is used effectively in the portraits of Lieutenant General James Parker DSM by Pat Whelan and Lieutenant General Patrick A. Mulcahy by James Le Jeune. As with the portrait of Collins, both pictures depict the figure standing against a typically Irish setting, a motif that establishes a symbolic link between the sitter and the land itself. This visual connection between the individual and the country or State is also presented in the portraits of Lieutenant General Gerald O'Sullivan DSM by John Coyle and Major General Patrick Delaney by Richard A. Free. In these cases, Ireland is represented by the tricolour, which hangs behind the sitter. In the portrait of Lieutenant General Carl O'Sullivan DSM, Free has drawn attention to the sitter's association with McKee Barracks itself, depicting the sitter casually posing within the grounds of the building complex. The most direct reference to a sitter's achievements during their military career can be seen in the portrait of Lieutenant General Collins-Powell. The two cavalry armoured cars in the background of the portrait allude to his personal promotion of the use of modern military equipment in the Irish Army. A nephew of Michael Collins, Collins-Powell was the first Irish officer to undergo formal cavalry training, which he did in Fort Meade, USA in 1927. The vehicle to the rear is a Panhard armoured car, a type acquired for the Army in 1964 when Collins-Powell was Quartermaster General, after his service as Chief of Staff. The closer vehicle is the Rolls Royce armoured car that was escorting Michael Collins's vehicle when Collins's convoy was ambushed at Béal na mBláth.

The distinguished status and responsibility associated with the rank of Chief of Staff is also evoked in the more refined symbolism of the sitter's pose and expression. The first seventeen portraits are consistent in their presentation of the sitter in half length, but this format was broken by John Coyle, who portrayed Lieutenant General Noel Bergin DSM in three-quarter length, a format that has since been preferred. The majority of the sitters are portrayed standing and looking purposefully towards the horizon, while others are seated and address the viewer, confidently demanding attention. Lorne Campbell argues that the sitter's pose and, above all, the facial expression, are essential indicators of demeanour.[11] A closer inspection of the individual likenesses on display reveals an array of subtle expressions and idiosyncrasies of posture. These visual signs communicate to us the artist's perception and interpretation of the unique characters that lie behind the sitter's official role.

All portraits must of course be considered as works of art, and when interpreting the portrayal of personality and character it is important to balance what seems to be the presentation of facts with the manner in which those facts are represented. An unexpected assortment of visual styles and painting techniques is exhibited by the eighteen different artists represented in this collection. Traditionally the most conservative form of visual expression, portraits tend to reflect or conform to the aesthetic conventions and expectations of the particular period in which they are produced. The extent to which this is realised ultimately comes down to the particular creative approach of the individual artist. A selection of the works at McKee Barracks reveals an understanding and a familiarity, among some of the artists, with modern approaches to painting. The works of James Le Jeune and Murial Brandt in particular demonstrate a relatively experimental use of composition and technique for aesthetic effect. Le Jeune employed a distinctly energetic and painterly approach to the production of form and structure in his portrait of Lieutenant General Mulcahy. The figure and background are composed of thick, fluid brushstrokes, producing a visual effect that emphasises the symbolic connection between the sitter and the landscape. Brandt, in contrast, adopted a more reductive approach, rendering both the background and figure of Major General Egan in blocks of flat colour and simplified shapes. The painting betrays the artist's concern for the formal, aesthetic qualities of the picture, which are as significant to the success of the composition as the portrayal of an engaging likeness. In general, however, the Chief of Staff portraits reveal the tendency among Irish painters and their patrons to favour a more academic approach to portraiture. Many of the artists here focus on the documentary function of the genre and the representation of natural effects. This focus on realism is particularly evident in the more recent pieces by James Hanley and Conor Walton, who have both produced finely crafted works that emulate and preserve a decidedly traditional and academic approach to portraiture. While this lends the collection a visual consistency, it is also evocative of the mainly conservative attitudes and expectations that defined Irish painting for much of the twentieth century.

Although portraits can function as aesthetic works of art, it is rarely the primary stimulus behind their commissioning, display and reception. Richard Brilliant observes that, for the viewer, there is 'a great difficulty in thinking about [portraits] as art and not thinking about them primarily as something else, the person represented'.[12] Portraits are ultimately material objects, and one only has to consider the history of portrait collections and the motivations behind forming them to assess the status of the portrait as an artwork. For instance, when the National Portrait Gallery, London was founded in 1856, it adopted five rules of guidance, 'the most significant', Bodkin noted, was 'that which binds them "to look to the celebrity of the person represented rather than to the merit of the artist"'.[13] This is true of many portrait collections, including the Chief of Staff series, the primary function of which is to honour and commemorate the men who have held Ireland's most senior military position.

Portraits have been used for a variety of commemorative, dynastic, personal and propagandist purposes throughout history.[14] Indeed, Shearer West observes that portraits, more than any other genre, 'draw attention to themselves as objects that can be employed or exploited in a variety of ways'.[15] Although it seems that the function of a portrait is primarily linked to the identity of sitter, portraits of the same individual can evoke very different interpretations, depending on the context and format in which they are presented. A portrait miniature, for instance, will inspire a more intimate interpretation than a portrait of the same individual that is exhibited publicly.

The Chief of Staff portraits hang side by side on the walls of the Officers' Mess. Conceived as a collection, they continue to develop as a cohesive series that reflects the organisation and traditions particular to this military institution. While the representation and documentation of the individual personalities is an important aspect of the series, assessed within the context of the collection, the works also inspire a more collective interpretation of national significance. Writing on national portrait collections, Fintan Cullen observes that the basis for such a collection 'is not just the accuracy of the features of a subject', but rather it is 'what the portrait represents'.[16] The decision to emphasise the historical importance of the sitter over the aesthetic quality of the artworks stresses the national and historical significance of the Chief of Staff collection. Indeed, on occasion, the Chief of Staff Portrait Committee relied on the skills of Maurice F. Cogan, and Peter Weafer, both officers serving in the barracks. In a sense, the collection presents the individual sitters as artefacts, in that they 'suggest memories and declare a history'.[17] It is both a collection of art and one that documents Ireland's military history.

The visual portrayal of military leaders has a long tradition, and this collection draws on the connotations associated with military culture and the history of military portraiture. This history extends all the way back to the ancient world and the representations of powerful generals, carved in stone or cast in bronze. Indeed, some of the earliest examples of the art of portraiture are those heads of great leaders depicted in profile on the face of coins, such as Julius Caesar. While such images are now useful historical artefacts, their production once played an essential role in conveying political power and authority in society. As Shearer West observes, 'portraits operate as signifiers of the status of the individuals they represent'.[18] An effective portrait can stimulate a viewer's sense of respect and admiration for an individual's leadership or achievements. This inherent yet significant characteristic of the genre has been recognised and exploited by leaders throughout history.

The military portrait became a significant artistic genre in itself and many rulers and heads of state favoured the portrayal and promotion of their martial status. Indeed, as recently as 2010, the first official portrait of British princes William and Harry depicts the brothers in military uniform. During the eighteenth and nineteenth centuries, it became increasingly popular for high-ranking officers to celebrate and commemorate their successes in battle by commissioning their portrait. It was common for men going to war to have their portrait painted before leaving. These portraits, often in miniature, could be thought of as a sort of substitute for the individual during their absence, or as a commemoration if they failed to return.

The portrayal of military figures is especially prevalent in nations with grand military traditions, such as the United Kingdom and France, where it also provided a significant source of income for portrait artists, including great masters of western art such as Jean Auguste Dominique Ingres, Joshua Reynolds and Thomas Lawrence. Although modern democracies have replaced the monarchies and empires of the past, many nations continue to celebrate their military histories through portraiture and the military portrait remains an important feature of many national portrait collections. The United States of America takes great pride in honouring its significant military figures and the National Portrait Gallery, Smithsonian Institute holds an extensive collection of portraits of Chiefs of Staff (or equivalent) of the United States Army. Beginning with George Washington, it includes such notable figures as Ulysses S. Grant, William Tecumseh Sherman and John J. Pershing. This continues throughout the twentieth century, with the portrayal of famous generals such as Douglas MacArthur and Dwight D. Eisenhower. Although such portraits may not hold the same associations as those of European monarchs, as a collection, they attain a similarly symbolic function. Marianna Jenkins argues that the primary purpose of State portraiture is the evocation of those abstract principles for which the individual stands. In this case, it is for the foundation and preservation of the United States of America as a democratic republic.

One could form a similar interpretation of the portraits at McKee Barracks. However, under the command of its Chiefs of Staff, the Irish military, as an organisation, has forged a very different identity to its US counterpart. The collection reflects this and, concealed within the walls of the Barracks, it has acquired a modest, unassuming presence within the visual culture of our society. As with the Irish Defence Forces, it does not court public attention, yet its role in the history of our State invites attention and respect. It is ironic, perhaps, that while many of the figures represented in the collection are relatively unfamiliar to the Irish public, their influence and the impact of their decisions has been felt in many remote areas of the globe. As the Irish Defence Forces has established a more international role, it has actively represented Ireland among communities that are often unfamiliar with our people and culture. In a sense, while our Defence Forces now operate within the international community of armed forces, as with each of the sitters that comprise this collection, it retains its own unique reputation and character, one that not only reflects the nature of the organisation, but which evokes the personality and identity of the Irish people.

Mr Donal Maguire, Administrator of the Centre for the study of Irish Art at the National Gallery of Ireland

THE OFFICE OF THE CHIEF OF STAFF IN HISTORICAL PERSPECTIVE

I AM GRATEFUL to Colonel Tom Hodson (Retd) and his colleagues for this opportunity to write about the Chiefs of Staff of the Defence Forces, and for allowing me complete freedom in what I write. I must also thank the current Chief of Staff, Lieutenant General Sean McCann, and Commandant Victor Laing of the Military Archives of Ireland for their help.

I offer few comments on contemporary military affairs, save to observe that the historical record of the State's management of defence affairs is not an encouraging one. Time and again, from the earliest days of the national Army's creation in 1922, there have been tensions between the military and civil sides of the defence establishment. These initially came to a head in the 'Army Crisis' of 1924, when a group of disaffected officers launched a half-hearted mutiny, which in substance amounted simply to deserting their posts and uttering bombastic threats formulated 'in a haze of whiskey'.[19] That crisis, resolved peacefully and with kid gloves, was followed by an acceleration of the demobilisation which had led to the unrest. In 1923, Army numbers stood at over 50,000 men; by 1928, total strength, including a small shambolic air arm, was about 7,000. Thereafter, the Defence Forces have, with the exception of the years from 1939 to 1945, been treated by the State with what can best be termed a combination of benign neglect and subliminal fear of the emergence of a generalissimo mentality which might someday see the Army seek to intervene in politics. This is reflected in the perpetuation of a culture of neurotic civil control of every aspect of defence affairs.

Repeatedly, reviews such as those by the Devlin Group in the 1960s, by the Gleeson Committee on Defence Forces' remuneration of 1989, and by external consultants in the 1990s, have pointed to significant weaknesses in the structures and practices of civil oversight of military affairs, resulting in duplication, indecision, confusion, delay and counterproductive second-guessing in even the most minor and mundane matters.

A number of factors, particularly the appearance of the State's first White Paper on Defence in 2000, and significant efforts to implement its modest ambitions over the succeeding decade, suggested that the primordial fear of an almighty military that underpinned the State's management of defence affairs since the 1924 mutiny is beginning to fade.[20] But there remain fundamental problems in defence affairs which run deeper than shortages of cash or organisational incoherence within the Defence Forces, important as those problems are.

One remarkable feature of Ireland's defence configuration, given her geographical position as an Atlantic island hundreds of miles west of mainland Europe, and shielded from the European mainland by Great Britain, is the subordination in defence organisation and thinking of air and sea defence. This is reflected in the career paths of Chiefs of Staff, only one of whom had any knowledge of aviation. This was P.A. Mulcahy (1955-8), whose undistinguished time as O/C of the Air Corps encompassed the humiliation of a committee of investigation in 1941-2, which uncovered a risible lack of professionalism, partly attributable to the fact that since the death of Michael Collins no one in senior command at GHQ had any focused ideas of what practical uses could be made of an air arm.[21] The situation is even starker in naval affairs: despite the decisive contribution of sea transport to the State's military operations during the Civil War, once that conflict was over plans for a permanent naval service were shelved. A small and ill-equipped service was eventually formed in 1946, but it was only with EEC entry in the 1970s, and after three decades of ineffectual farce, that a functional coastal patrol arm was developed. Unlike analogues in comparable, small, maritime states, the Irish naval service still appears to exist in an entirely separate sphere to land forces, with the very occasional exception of logistical support for overseas missions. To what extent Chiefs of Staff have any responsibility for this state of affairs remains irrelevant, but no holder of that post has had any significant naval training or experience.

The very term 'Defence Forces' indicates an organisational plurality which undoubtedly adds complexity while militating against overall efficiency and interoperability, and renders the State's air and naval arms 'Cinderella services', even in comparison with her very modest land forces. It would surely make more strategic and organisational sense, particularly for an island nation, to have a unitary 'defence force' of three interoperable arms (as was achieved in Australia with the creation of the Australian Defence Force as a joint services organisation in 1976).[22]

A prime example of enduring dysfunctionality is the formal relationship between the Defence Forces and the government. In legislative terms, the Council of Defence sits proudly at the apex of civil military dealings, as the mechanism through which the government exercises control of the Defence Forces and takes counsel on military affairs. According to the Defence Forces website, this body is currently comprised of the 'Minister of State' at the Department of Defence (there is no such junior minister at present), the Secretary General of the department, the Chief of Staff, and the two deputy chiefs. Yet the council exists only in statute law and on organisation charts; even at times of crisis with enormous security implications, such as the Emergency of 1939-45, or the outbreak of serious civil unrest in Northern Ireland in 1969, it lay dormant. The Devlin Group on public service reorganisation of 1966-9 made one key recommendation regarding defence matters, namely that the Council of Defence should, as the law plainly anticipated, meet regularly and serve as the highest interface between the military professionals and the civilian policy system. Four decades later, that has yet to happen.

Such enduring dysfunctionality cannot simply be a matter of neglect. I think it reflects institutionalised distrust within civil government of a potentially overweening Army. Yet the very disinclination to operate a coherent and regularised procedure for deliberating on and managing defence affairs contributed to the 'arms crisis' of 1970, a calamity alike for the Defence Forces and for the State. Had the processes for managing civil/military interaction laid down by law been in operation, it seems unlikely that the Army would have found itself in such a quagmire. The arms crisis threw up such issues as how the government directed the Defence Forces, and how professional military advice was provided to and considered by ministers; it also highlighted the problematic question of whether any Chief of Staff could actually exercise overall control of the Defence Forces. The crisis did damage to the standing of the Defence Forces, suggesting that the Army was open to irregular political interference. It thus refreshed the withered roots of fears about military involvement in political affairs, and it continues to cast a shadow.

CHIEFS OF STAFF AND THE DEFENCE FORCES
DURING THE STATE'S FORMATIVE YEARS

The effective role of the Chief of Staff has varied considerably, usually as a function of factors outside the control of individual incumbents. Chiefs of Staff have had to discharge their duties in often challenging and uncertain circumstances. The formal structures and processes through which defence affairs are deliberated on and decided at government level do not fully capture the complexities and nuances of civil/military relations.

The Chief of Staff has far wider responsibilities of leadership, co-ordination and tendering professional advice to the government than he has effective powers to discharge them. He is formally at most, to borrow Brian Farrell's typology for heads of Irish governments since independence, a 'chairman' rather than a 'chief'.[23] He has no power of direct command over troops, and while both statute and custom enjoin him to be the State's principal military advisor, and thus the key interface between the Defence Forces and the policy system, officers just below him in the defence hierarchy have always had independent access to the Minister for Defence. Furthermore, as we have seen, the statutory framework under which Chiefs of Staff operate bears little relation to realities.

The extent of Richard Mulcahy's influence and control as Chief of Staff during the War of Independence remains a moot point. Many of the most active IRA leaders looked to Michael Collins for direction and support, and ascribed to Collins personally decisions and actions which in fact may have arisen elsewhere in GHQ. Mulcahy was himself an active and demanding figure, always eager to know about events on the ground and never slow to admonish, to criticise and to attempt to draw the appropriate military lessons from setbacks as well as from victories. His willingness to ask hard questions earned him few friends, and possibly contributed to the marked tendency amongst IRA officers outside Dublin to ascribe everything useful done by GHQ to Collins personally. It is clear that GHQ consistently sought to provide direction and encouragement to the IRA throughout the country, and that by 1921 they were succeeding in establishing a measure of control and in imposing a general concept of war aims and methods. This was so in terms of establishing general policy, of supplying weapons, and of dispatching organisers to ginger up quiet areas like Cavan or to provide advice and guidance to places like South Tipperary, where there was a clear willingness to fight. The GHQ records in the Mulcahy papers show that some units responded far more fully than others to Dublin's strictures, directives and requests. What always mattered most on the ground, however, were weapons and ammunition, not fatuous documents such as the 'Training Order' issued on 1 July 1921, which instructed all O/Cs to ensure 'that all Officers, NCO and men are able to swim'.[24]

Nevertheless, it is clear that by the time of the truce in July 1921, GHQ was achieving its aim of creating a coherent, layered military structure, enabling it to exercise direction and control over the IRA generally. It was the pre-truce GHQ which provided the template and many of the personnel for defence headquarters when the national Army was formed in the early months of 1922, and once Civil War broke out on 28 June 1922, it was GHQ which oversaw and controlled the provisional government's very effective military response. Despite possessing a preponderance of hardened fighters at local level, the anti-Treaty forces were out-generalled rather than simply overwhelmed by force of numbers. Using all its advantages of resources and communications, GHQ planned and fought an effective campaign, which within two months saw the provisional government in control of all significant towns and ports. Despite problems of indiscipline, and worse, thanks to GHQ's control, the new State's Army quickly triumphed over the anti-Treaty IRA. The new Army's reward was to be subjected to a process of force reduction and defence expenditure so drastic as to render it, within a decade, little more than a poorly armed *gendarmerie* of uncertain efficiency and purpose, but, crucially, of absolute loyalty to the State.

BECOMING CHIEF: CAREER PATHS UP TO THE 1960S

The qualities, record and qualifications required for holders of the office of Chief of Staff have changed markedly over the decades. There persists a belief that, historically, political factors greatly influenced many senior and not-so-senior appointments within the Defence Forces, particularly prior to the establishment of modern processes for merit-based selection of senior officers. This is something impossible to document.

Men appointed since the 1970s have invariably had experience on United Nations or other international missions, have significant staff college training (sometimes gained abroad), and often have university degrees. Things were very different up to the 1960s, as academic and staff qualifications were conspicuous by their absence. Only one chief, Liam Egan (1952-4), held a university degree on appointment (a BA in English and French acquired before he joined the IRA). He was also the first to have attended staff college abroad – he was a member of the military mission sent to the United States under Colonel Hugo McNeill in 1926-7 for advanced officer training, a preamble to Army reorganisation. Richard Mulcahy (1918-21 and 1922-3) was briefly a medical student after the 1916 Rising, but soon abandoned his studies for full-time revolutionary work.

Experience took the place of educational qualifications. Until 1960, all Chiefs of Staff had War of Independence and Civil War experience, and one – P.A. Mulcahy (1955-60) – had also served in the British Army during the First World War. At least two – Michael Brennan (1931-40) and Liam Archer (1949-52) – bore the scars of battle (Brennan had gunshot wounds to his arm; Archer had lost a toe in 1916).

There are no other common denominators. Horsemanship was an attribute valued amongst officers (resulting in the emergence of a complex set of rules governing the quartering and care of privately owned and exercised officers' horses, of privately owned horses sometimes used for official Army purposes, and of Army-owned horses sometimes used inappropriately for private business, which kept the Dáil committee of public accounts busy from time to time).[25] I have been unable to ascertain who was the last Chief of Staff to appear mounted on official duties, but ability to ride a horse is no longer, if it ever was, a requirement for holders of the office.

Yet a horse does feature in the perhaps apocryphal explanation given by de Valera's authorised biographers for the appointment as Chief of Staff, in the midst of acute crisis in January 1940, of Colonel Dan McKenna. McKenna had previously impressed de Valera with his coolness and capacity, when he led a party on horseback to rescue the snowbound Taoiseach from a cottage in the Dublin mountains.[26] It is clear that, while down the pecking order in terms of rank – McKenna was only deputy quartermaster general, a post in which he had recently been installed precisely to bring life to a comatosed organisational function – he already had an outstanding record as a professional soldier. Born in County Derry, where he had commanded an IRA battalion during the War of Independence, he earned the reputation not simply of a particularly dedicated and able officer, but, unusually in a very small force dominated by old salts proud of their individual fighting records, of one not afraid to speak his mind, even when this led to difficulties with superiors. When asked in 1925 to record his views on the Provisional Government's pre-Civil War approach to northern affairs in 1922, McKenna expressed trenchant and well-considered criticism, arguing that the policy of encouraging northern nationalists to effectively boycott the new northern State and its administrative and political structures had contributed to their isolation by the Belfast regime. In an emaciated Army with an officer corps largely cowed by fear of political disfavour, he stood out for his forthrightness. As Chief of Staff he could be terrifying: the late Colonel Dan Bryan recalled hearing him, within hours of his appointment, savaging a senior officer for a dilatory and defeatist attitude.[27]

No subsequent Chief of Staff has remotely had the opportunities bestowed on McKenna by the presence of major internal and external threats of invasion and subversion. This is not to downplay his personal achievement: he seized the opportunities which circumstances offered to build a credible two-division Army more or less from scratch, and to brief the government in no uncertain terms on long-term issues. From June 1940, McKenna and senior officers were permitted to engage in increasingly frank discussions with British forces about joint defence of the island of Ireland. Initially chaperoned by the secretary of the Department of External Affairs, such vital professional contacts were soon left entirely in his own hands (with the exception of security and intelligence liaisons with the British and Americans, which were conducted by director Colonel Dan Bryan under the watchful eyes of External Affairs). The confidence placed in McKenna, and the relatively free hand accorded him, enabled him to speak his mind not only to his subordinates, but to his political masters. What other Chief of Staff would have dared even to think of proposing the introduction of compulsory national service, still less to point out that it offered the only way forward after 1945 for the State to maintain Defence Forces capable of mounting more than symbolic resistance to external aggression?[28]

McKenna's immediate successors after his retirement in 1949 also had 'national records', but circumstances rendered them far less powerful within the Defence Forces and in their dealings with the State. The last Chief of Staff with direct War of Independence or Civil War experience was Sean Collins-Powell, who served in 1961-2, while Lieutenant General Sean McKeown DSM was commanding ONUC in the Congo.

In considering the significance of 1916-23 records for Chiefs of Staff during the first four decades of independence, we should note that amongst ministers such experience was even longer lived. Richard Mulcahy acted both as Chief of Staff and Minister for Defence in 1922-4, and, after the death of Michael Collins in August 1922, assumed the additional role of Commander-in-Chief until the end of the Civil War. With the exception of four years after his enforced resignation in 1924, he served in every Cumann na nGaedheal/Fine Gael government up to 1957. Sean MacEoin followed his brief time as Chief of Staff in 1929 with two stints as Minister for Defence, briefly in 1951 and again from 1954 to 1957. Frank Aiken, Minister for Defence from 1932 to 1939, and Minister for the Co-ordination of Defensive Measures from 1939 to 1945, had succeeded Liam Lynch as IRA Chief of Staff in May 1923, before eventually following de Valera into constitutional political life. He served in all Fianna Fáil cabinets until 1969. Oscar Traynor, Minister for Defence from 1939 to 1948 and from 1951 to 1954, had been O/C Dublin Brigade during the War of Independence and the Civil War. He was in all Fianna Fáil cabinets until 1961. Michael Hilliard of Meath, Minister for Defence from 1965 to 1969, was also a War of Independence and Civil War veteran. At the highest political level, Sean

Lemass, Taoiseach from 1959 to 1966, was a 1916-23 man. His successor, Jack Lynch was the first Taoiseach without a 'national record', marking a generational break. But we might note that Lynch's immediate successors as Taoiseach, Charles Haughey and Garret FitzGerald, both had direct experience of military life from their student days in the Pearse Battalion in University College Dublin.

Finally, we should also note that the civil service side of the Department of Defence, established in 1922, was not without direct military expertise, something which proved a double-edged sword for the new Army. The first secretary of the department, Charles O'Connor (1922-7), was a highly decorated British Army veteran. His successor, Peadar MacMahon (1927-58), had War of Independence and Civil War experience, and had been appointed Chief of Staff after the Army mutiny. Whatever his personal qualities, MacMahon's translation to the civil side of Defence made him a poacher-turned-gamekeeper. Successive Chiefs of Staff were consequently in a very difficult position *vis à vis* the department. Under MacMahon, Defence had two overriding priorities: the first, in the wake of the 1924 mutiny, was to ensure that the Army never again attempted to defy the civil power; the second, arising partly from the chaotic manner in which the new Army had mushroomed during the Civil War and the nightmarish administrative challenges presented by successive military service pensions laws covering service in 1916, the War of Independence and eventually the Civil War, was to maintain an iron grip on expenditure. There is little evidence in succeeding decades of any strategic thinking within the department about national defence policy prior to the production, in 2000, of the welcome though anodyne White Paper on Defence. What mattered after 1924 was that the Army was kept subdued, that as little public money as possible was spent on it, and that it was just large and effective enough both to provide a simulacrum of a national defence force, and to counter the continued internal republican threat to the State.

The sheer continuity of experience over almost five decades within the national defence establishment is in curious contrast to the State's main internal foe, the IRA. The last IRA Chief of Staff with any War of Independence or Civil War experience was Stephen Hayes, deposed and court-martialled in 1941. Thereafter, the IRA, in its various mutations, was headed by a succession of men too young to have played any part in the conflict which saw the establishment and consolidation of independent Ireland.

We may ask why, given that the administrative and political elites up to the 1970s contained many with fighting experience from the 1916-32 era, defence matters were so dismally neglected in independent Ireland. One of the principal reasons – distrust of an almighty Army – has already been discussed. Another, however, relates specifically to the kind of action to which Irish separatists had been exposed. Theirs was a sporadic insurgency, not a conventional war. Furthermore, such combat as there was took place entirely on land: neither air nor sea operations played a frontline role at any point (save, perhaps, the shelling of Liberty Hall by HMS *Helga* in 1916, the occasional use of aircraft for communications and observation purposes by the British during the War of Independence and by government forces during the Civil War, and the decisive use of ships to move government troops rapidly around the coastline in 1922-3). It is, therefore, perhaps not surprising that air and maritime defence issues received even less attention than military matters on land.

Precipitate Departures of Chiefs of Staff

A key question for any Chief of Staff is how to manage relations with the civil side of Defence and with the Army's political masters. History suggests that this is a difficult task.

On the civil side of the government machine, where at any one time during the fifty years up to 1971 there were perhaps twenty people holding secretary of department rank, the total number of enforced departures from public service, or resignations on principle was just two (and one of these men, Dan O'Donovan, was later effectively reinstated). In the civil sphere, however great the principle dividing an official from his minister, or however egregious the failings of a department or State agency, the man at the top could almost always stay nominally in situ, even if effectively bypassed. In contrast, of the far smaller numbers of professional heads of the Defence Forces up to 1971, we know that at least two were consciously dispensed with against their will, while two other early Chiefs of Staff departed very quickly of their own volition.

In 1924, General Sean MacMahon was dismissed in the aftermath of the Army mutiny after he had queried the government's demand for his resignation. His minister, Richard Mulcahy, and the other members of the Army council resigned. MacMahon could scarcely be blamed for the mutiny, given the faction-ridden force which he inherited and the incurable indiscipline of a coterie of discontented officers with significant political connections and protectors. In accepting his fate, MacMahon vindicated the principle that the Army must obey the lawful commands of the government. He was rehabilitated later in 1924, being reappointed to GOC rank, but he retired soon afterwards on health grounds. In 1929, Dan Hogan resigned suddenly after less than two years as Chief of Staff, most likely for personal reasons, and departed from Ireland for good. His successor, Sean MacEoin, served for just a few months before resigning in order to contest (and win) a Dáil by-election as a government supporter. His successor, Joseph Sweeney, lasted only two years, being superseded by Michael Brennan in October 1931, although remaining in the Army as a command O/C until December 1940.

Brennan's appointment in October 1931 brought unexpected stability to the office of Chief of Staff. It was widely anticipated that he would be forced out on political grounds after Fianna Fáil took power in March 1932, but his outstanding War of Independence record, and his reputation for clean fighting during the Civil War, made him acceptable to the new regime. His first Minister of Defence was Frank Aiken, who as IRA Chief of Staff in May 1923 had issued the 'dump arms' order which brought the Civil War to an end. Brennan played a very important role in securing a peaceful transfer of power from the Civil War victors to the losers, and his three-year term of office was twice renewed by de Valera's government. He was superseded in January 1940, just days after the humiliation of the IRA's Magazine Fort raid, in which almost all the Army's small arms ammunition reserves were stolen. In fact, the government had decided some weeks previously to replace him, as it was thought that fresh blood was needed to galvanise the Army in the altered circumstances of a general European war. Brennan, still a young man with a young family, was found a civilian post and was left no worse off financially.

In the humdrum post-war decades, the office of Chief of Staff became a single-term appointment, resulting in the curiosity that a number of departing Chiefs, instead of collecting a gold watch and a handshake and taking dignified retirement, were simply posted elsewhere in the Army. This can hardly have strengthened the authority of their successors; nor can it have done much for the morale of other officers who had aspired to general rank.

CONCLUSION

The professional backgrounds of Chiefs of Staff have changed radically over the last fifty years. In the four decades up to 1960, all holders of the office had direct experience of combat; some, such as Michael Brennan, had killed people, and at least two had been badly wounded in action. Only one held a university degree or had received staff college training abroad. By contrast, in recent decades, all Chiefs of Staff have undergone extensive professional training throughout their careers – indeed, most have been staff college instructors at one time or another – while their personal experience of combat has been acquired outside Ireland on United Nations or other international peacekeeping duties.

The international dimension of Irish military service apart, the challenges of the post have remained largely unchanged in the modern era. The structure for civil military engagement laid down by the Oireachtas simply does not operate. Compared with his analogues in other small democracies, an Irish Chief of Staff has very limited direct control over the Defence Forces of which he is the professional head. A Chief of Staff has to operate in a politico-bureaucratic minefield, where the most abstruse and technical questions may be taken out of professional hands and decided on the basis of potential political ramifications, not of military needs and effectiveness. Yet, fortunately for Ireland, people can still be found who will accept this challenging job and who will try to do it well.

Professor Eunan O'Halpin, Centre for Contemporary Irish History, Trinity College Dublin

THE SITTER AND THE ARTIST

THE PORTRAITS of Chiefs of Staffs held in McKee Barracks Officers' Mess represent a history of the Defence Forces on canvas. The collection's symbolic significance is part biographical, part cultural and part tribute to those who have commanded the Defences Forces over the decades. It not only contributes to the military iconography of the State, but is an important element in Ireland's artistic heritage. Officers draw pride and inspiration from the sequence and aspire to be part of it; equally, artists are anxious to be associated with it. Although each painter brings a unique decorative style and technical expression to the collection, he must be true to both the individual personality of the sitter and the heritage of the Defence Forces.

Lieutenant General Colm E. Mangan DSM retired as Chief of Staff in 2004 and the Defence Forces commissioned James Hanley RHA as his official portrait artist. This was an important milestone in the careers of both men. Their observations, thoughts and recollections are now outlined.

THE SITTER: LIEUTENANT GENERAL COLM E. MANGAN DSM

In early 2003, my Aide, Captain Stephen Ryan, announced, 'Sir, it's time to decide on your portrait for the Mess.' I was completely taken aback. I was not due to retire for over a year and had given no thought to the administrative details of retirement or indeed any aspect of it. My first reaction was to ignore it – maybe the whole process would simply go away. However, Stephen was having none of it. I had to face up to the prospects of life out of uniform after forty-four years of service and my portrait was to be the first step.

All through my career, as both a young officer and a not-so-young officer, I sat with my peers in the dining room of the Officers' Mess in McKee Barracks and joked about the portraits, or 'rogues gallery', that adorned the walls. These 'rogues' were my predecessors as Chief of Staff and my retirement meant that the time had come to join their ranks. In effect, I was now exposing myself to the sort of ribald commentary in which I had indulged for so long. This last thought brought home to me the importance of getting the best possible painter for the portrait, so that as far as possible, the excellence of the work might divert criticism of the subject. Of particular concern was the knowledge that the picture would remain in the dining room for about twenty-seven years, given that every time a Chief of Staff retires, one portrait relocates to the corridor to make room for the 'gallery's' latest candidate. Consequently, every three to four years, a form of musical chairs is played as a new Chief arrives to take the heat off the others.

Steve had done a lot of research and presented me with a selection of painters and photographs of their work. After much soul-searching, we decided on James Hanley RHA and a meeting with him was arranged, so as to discuss the details of sittings, etc. I was relieved to discover that I would only have to 'sit' for one or two sessions, during which James would make the sketches and take the photographs needed to do the portrait. A few weeks later, James returned to Defence Forces Headquarters with all his artist's gear and took photographs both in the office and in the grounds of the building. A seated pose was decided upon, with James even supplying a rather comfortable chair for that purpose. From time to time he returned for some final sketching and to check fine details. The whole process was surprisingly relaxing and trouble free. I enjoyed talking to James as he worked; he has a genuine interest in both Irish history and the Defence Forces. As always in the military, dress became an issue. I was particularly keen on one picture taken by James of me wearing Combat Uniform and felt it would make an excellent painting. This was given the thumbs down by my

ADC on the grounds of tradition. Reluctantly, I accepted this point, so Service Dress No. 1 it had to be! However, I was not to be denied my personal choice, and I commissioned James privately to paint it. Today it commands pride of place in my Naas home.

Retirement was set for 21 February 2004 and some weeks before that date I was given a preview of the portrait. I was very pleased with it, but naturally was anxious to see what my family and colleagues would make of it at the unveiling. On the twenty-first, the general reaction was very favourable. I was fortunate that my mother was present at the ceremony; her critical faculties had not been impaired by her ninety-six years, which she wore lightly. 'That's not my son!' was her first reaction, 'That's just some general.' One of her grandchildren then piped up, 'But Granny, maybe that's the way the Army see him.'

'Maybe,' she replied, but she didn't seem convinced.

Today, the portrait hangs in the dining room of the Officers' Mess in McKee Barracks. It has been moved on the first stage of the journey around the wall and it will eventually wind up in the corridor. I'd like to think that I would see it there, but I'm afraid the time and space calculations make that impossible. So maybe I'll settle for a place in the enclosure past Douglas Hyde.

THE ARTIST: JAMES HANLEY RHA

In 2003 I was invited to submit slides and a costing to Captain Stephen Ryan, the ADC to the Chief of Staff at the time, Lieutenant General Colm E. Mangan DSM, potentially to paint the retirement portrait of the Chief of Staff for the Officers' Mess, McKee Barracks. I was very happy, thereafter, to get the news that I had been selected for the job. As a portrait painter, the chance to paint a military subject was a great opportunity, particularly allied to the proud history of the Defence Forces, and my own passionate interest in the founder of the Free State Army, General Michael Collins, whose portrait also hangs in the McKee Officers' Mess.

The Collins portrait, painted posthumously by Leo Whelan RHA in the 1940s, is a copy of his own State portrait of Collins which hangs in Leinster House, and which was painted from a photograph of Collins at Arthur Griffith's funeral, a week before Collins himself was shot in Cork. Hands clasped in military gloves, Collins stands strong against a romantic sky, removed from the context of the original source to look heroic and dramatic, as befits the myth of this formidable military and political figure. The next portrait in the series always hangs next to the Leo Whelan painting, and I was immediately conscious of comparisons. I examined the idea of the appropriateness of the Whelan portrait as a template for a contemporary portrait of a general commanding a Defence Forces which has been lauded worldwide, since its inception, for its peacekeeping role.

To counteract and complement the Whelan portrait, Lieutenant General Mangan agreed to be seated, which differed from the majority of the previous portraits (many are half length, so it is not possible to determine if they are in fact seated or standing). The general posed without his cap, which he felt was more appropriate for the seated pose, which also showed him in a three quarters angle, which I felt was his most distinctive look. In this relaxed and yet strong and authentic pose, Lieutenant General Mangan's characteristics as a tall and fit man come across, even while seated. The background colour is a blue shade which I frequently use. In this instance, the colour was particularly appropriate, as it represents the outdoor life of a soldier and is also a nod to the long service with United Nations peacekeeping. I included the crest of the Defence Forces, something close to Lieutenant General Mangan's heart, as well as the tricolour, representing the national aspect of the office.

Initially, Lieutenant General Mangan did express an interest in breaking with tradition and being painted in DPM, which he felt might reflect his more day-to-day activities as a soldier and leader. However, after some reflection, he decided against it. I did paint a private commission for him in his DPMs as a happy compromise. There is only one other deviation from the norm in the McKee Barracks collection, where Lieutenant General T.L. O'Carroll is painted in dress uniform.

I was ambitious to paint a life-size, three-quarter-length portrait – one that naturally couldn't be as big as the Collins painting and also that wouldn't be too obviously bigger than some of the more modestly (and disparately) sized portraits of the past. This caused me some concern, in that I didn't want the painting to be seen as 'political' in any way, but I felt that a substantial size is no more than the office itself deserved. I do feel vindicated to a degree; when one sees the two portraits of Chiefs of Staff I have done, along with Conor Walton's recent painting of Lieutenant General Sreenan, it is clear that a 'uniform' (no pun intended) size is more fitting, more harmonious to the cycle of work in the collection and more suitable to the proportions of the room in which these paintings hang.

Finally, the portrait was a good exercise in getting all the detail correct of the uniform – a fascinating process for me. Making sure the medal sequence, the flash, insignia, Sam Browne belt, name plate, buttons and fabric colour, etc., were all present and correct was an education, as well as a duty to the career of the man I was painting, and an integral element of the tradition of the portrait sequence to which my painting now proudly belongs.

Lieutenant General Colm Mangan DSM (Retd) and James Hanley RHA

REFLECTIONS ON THE MCKEE BARRACKS PORTRAIT COLLECTION

THE DESIRE for immortality has been an aspect of human nature from earliest times. The great German artist of the fifteenth century, Albrecht Dürer drew and painted portraits with extraordinary insight and skill, believing that 'portraiture preserves the look of people after their deaths'. He illustrated his point by drawing a harrowing charcoal head and shoulders portrait of his mother in old age, where every wrinkle and blemish was included, to leave posterity with an unforgettable image of a dignified old lady about to meet her death. He was equally skilful painting in oils, leaving behind him a youthful, serious self-portrait that not only tells us what he looked like, but also illustrates the clothes that he wore and the expression of high intelligence that was his inheritance. Dürer was succeeded by many other great masters of portraiture in the centuries that followed, including Hans Holbein, Rembrandt Van Rijn, Anthony Van Dyck, Peter Lely, Godfrey Kneller, Joshua Reynolds, Thomas Gainsborough, and a host of lesser practitioners thereafter.

By the nineteenth century, portraiture had in all probability become the dominant art form in Britain and Ireland. Kings and queens, Church leaders, Army generals, even politicians and members of the rich merchant classes were commissioning prominent artists of the day to paint their portraits, to proclaim their importance and success in life, and to ensure their places in history. Gentlemen's clubs such as The Cavalry & Guards Club, The Athenaeum Club and The Garrick Club in London began to accept and then commission portraits of prominent members for display in their exclusive premises. Thomas Lawrence PRA painted flamboyant, flattering portraits of gentry to hang in these institutions. Winners of Nobel prizes such as Sir John Cockcroft and Rudyard Kipling sat for portrait painters by popular demand. A host of portrait miniature painters flourished in Britain and Ireland, finding customers among Army officers *en route* to India and the ladies they left behind, of whom they needed visual reminders.

In Ireland at the end of the nineteenth century, Walter Osborne RHA, Sarah Purser HRHA and John Butler Yeats RHA were prominently painting portraits to earn a living. They were soon joined by the prodigy William Orpen HRHA, RA, who displayed exceptional talent at the Metropolitan School of Art before departing for London, where he earned a fortune for many years afterwards, painting vivid portraits of the rich and famous, though he was equally adept at painting landscape and genre scenes. Luckily for Ireland, he came back for a short time annually to teach at the Metropolitan School of Art, where some of his most distinguished pupils were Seán Keating PRHA, Patrick Tuohy RHA and Leo Whelan RHA, all of whom later painted important Irish portraits. They in turn, became teachers themselves and the dominant influence was the South Kensington School of realistic portraiture as practised by Orpen, Tonks, Rothenstein and other English painters at that time. The more colourful, less inhibited style of occasional portrait painting practised in France at that time by *avant-garde* artists such as Vincent Van Gogh, Auguste Renoir, Pablo Picasso and Henri Matisse seemed to have no influence on painters who remained in Ireland, though their influence was obvious on painters who visited France regularly including Roderic O'Conor, W. J. Leech, John Lavery and Mary Swanzy, all of whom painted portraits from time to time, although they were not classified exclusively as portrait painters.

There are a number of collections of portraits in Ireland at the present time. Perhaps the most important collection of historic portraits is that of the twenty-two portraits of British royalty, Lord Lieutenants and Dukes, nineteen of which still hang in the Great Hall of the Royal Hospital Kilmainham. These were taken over by the Irish Free State in 1922, after the British administration had departed. They are looked after today by the Office of Public Works but are not being added to, for obvious reasons.

Likewise, there are historical portraits in Dublin Castle, inherited from British times, though suitable additions have been made, through purchase, to this collection in recent years. Trinity College Dublin also has an important collection of formal portraits, mostly of provosts down through the centuries, from the foundation of the college in 1592 by Queen Elizabeth I. The college also possesses an attractive portrait of the Virgin Queen herself. What is particularly interesting about the Trinity collection is that the authorities there keep adding to it on a regular basis by commissioning living Irish artists to paint prominent office holders such as provosts, chancellors and professors, in the way that the Irish Army at McKee Barracks in Dublin records its successive Chiefs of Staff. The collection of portraits of Chiefs of Staff of the Irish Army only came into being in 1950. It was a courageous and far-sighted initiative of the Army at that time. McKee Barracks itself is a most attractive architectural masterpiece in red brick, which was once rumoured to have been designed for India and built in Dublin by mistake. I am sure there is no foundation for this suggestion, in reality, but it was current in circulation many years ago, perhaps for obvious reasons. Its collection to date numbers twenty-seven portraits, the latest being the portrait by James Hanley RHA, of the late Lieutenant General Dermot Earley DSM, an outstanding sportsman in his youth, who passed away all too soon after his recent retirement from the Army as a most popular Chief of Staff.

The portraits hang in roughly chronological order on the walls of the Officers' Mess of McKee Barracks. They add greatly to its decoration and attractiveness. The commissioned Chiefs of Staff portraits are accompanied by a few other related portraits, perhaps the finest of which is a portrait of Dr Douglas Hyde, stylishly painted by Seán O'Sullivan RHA. Douglas Hyde was a poet and sportsman as well as an enthusiastic Gaelic scholar. The portrait reveals him to have become somewhat portly in his maturity, but yet distinguished in appearance, with a prominent forehead and handlebar moustache. It suggests a man with a lively, likeable personality and a zest for life and love of his country. It is recorded that An Taoisech Éamon de Valera and several government ministers attended a dinner in 1944 in Áras an Uachtaráin hosted by President Hyde. The portrait of the President by Seán O'Sullivan was on view, commissioned by the Office of the President for presentation to the Army. The Taoiseach then expressed the view that it should be accepted as a general principle that a portrait of every President should be painted and hung in the Áras. The proposal was soon afterwards approved by government, and Leo Whelan RHA was immediately commissioned to paint the official portrait of President Hyde. The finished work was collected by the Office of Public Works from the artist's studio in 1945 and has since been on display in Áras an Uachtaráin, being the first in a line of successive portraits of Presidents. The President is portrayed standing, three-quarter length, dressed in formal dark suit and holding a roll of parchment in his hand. Thus was the protocol established for succeeding Presidents of Ireland, whose portraits have all been commissioned by the Office of Public Works from leading Irish artists and hung in the formal rooms of the residence in the Phoenix Park.

The first Chief of Staff, or Commander-in-Chief as he was then designated, of the Irish Army was the ebullient, extraordinary leader General Michael Collins from County Cork, who was so central, with Éamon de Valera, to the founding of the Irish Free State. His life was tragically cut short when he was shot during an ambush by rival rebel forces at Béal na mBláth in 1922. The portrait, also by Leo Whelan RHA, is undated and is, almost certainly, a posthumous one painted by the artist from a photograph. General Collins is dressed in a smart green Irish Free State Army uniform with brass buttons, leather belt and brown gauntlets. He wears the peaked cap with the 'FF', Soldiers of Destiny, Army insignia, and is portrayed standing three-quarter length, looking to the left, against a background of a mottled grey-green sky and low hills in the distant background, probably recalling his native County Cork. It is an accomplished portrait of a man who exudes strength of character and steely determination. The McKee portrait was acquired from the artist in 1951 and bears a remarkable resemblance to a similar, undated portrait of Michael Collins presented to Leinster House in 1944 by a subscription committee. The latter, also by Leo Whelan RHA, hangs today in the front hall of Leinster House. There is also in existence a less-than-life-size bronze sculpture of Michael Collins in Farmleigh by Éamonn O' Doherty, which is most likely modelled after the portraits by Leo Whelan.

Leo Whelan was a contemporary of Seán Keating, Harry Clarke, Margaret Crilly and Patrick Tuohy at the Metropolitan School of Art. In the 1920s, he was somewhat overshadowed by Tuohy, who was then regarded by many as the leading Irish portrait painter and who was chosen by James Joyce to paint the Joyce family portraits. Tuohy's tragic death in New York in 1930 left the portrait field open to Whelan, who went on to paint many portraits of professional Irish people, including eminent physicians. Today, a number of these portraits adorn the walls of the Royal College of Physicians of Ireland on Kildare Street, Dublin.

In 1951, Leo Whelan was commissioned to paint the portrait of General Ristéard Mulcahy, the second Commander-in-Chief, for McKee Barracks. The result was an accomplished portrait very different in style and colouring to the large, grisaille, half-length portrait of the general painted by Patrick Tuohy in 1921, which is still in private ownership. A quick preparatory oil sketch of Mulcahy's head and shoulders by Tuohy was given to his pupil Maurice MacGonigal PRHA, whose son Ciarán later donated it to the National Gallery of Ireland. MacGonigal is also represented in the McKee Barracks collection by his portrait of Lieutenant General P. Mc Mahon, also painted in 1951. In addition, he was chosen by Taoiseach Seán Lemass to paint his official portrait for Leinster House.

All of the portraits in McKee Barracks are formal portraits, which is appropriate for such a cohesive collection. A more or less uniform canvas size has been set for commissioned portraits over the years and this is in keeping with government protocol for formal portraits of Taoisigh which hang in Leinster House. All of the portraits are painted in oil on canvas and are framed in similarly appropriate fashion. The Army sitters look extremely distinguished in their neatly pressed uniforms, and the portraits reinforce an impression of strong, highly intelligent men who have reached 'the top' of their profession through exceptional qualities of discipline and courageous leadership. They must also be a source of inspiration and pride to young officers serving in the Irish Army. Some of the Chiefs of Staff have led their troops into dangerous United Nations peacekeeping operations in Europe, Africa and Asia with outstanding results, albeit with some sad fatalities, as in the case of the Niemba Ambush in the Congo some decades ago. It must be every young cadet's ambition to someday rise to the top of the nation's armed forces, and to have his or her portrait commissioned by a leading Irish portrait artist to hang on the Mess walls in the distinguished line of succession. The point has to be made that so far no female officer has yet been appointed Chief of Staff of the Irish Army, but likewise no female has yet become Taoiseach of this nation, though we have had two female Presidents in the last two decades and their official portraits have been painted to hang in Áras an Uachtaráin in accordance with official protocol there.

The historic practice of having officers in the British Army sit for their portraits was widespread, but not unique to Britain. The United States of America has a collection of portraits of their Chiefs of Staff of the Armed Forces. Even today, some African nations have begun to commission and exhibit portraits of leading military figures at their Army Headquarters, despite the fact that painting on canvas was not historically widespread on that continent.

It was appropriate that the Irish Army should turn to the membership of the Royal Hibernian Academy in order to choose suitable artists to paint the portraits. The Academicians had all received traditional training in the theory and practice of drawing and painting, and were mostly well-equipped to undertake portrait commissions. It is not surprising, then, to discover that three past Presidents of the Academy feature among the painters of the Chiefs of Staff portraits. Seán Keating PPRHA, the star pupil of Orpen, painted the portrait of Major General M. Brennan in 1958 and General Eoin O'Duffy at an earlier date. Chief of Staff Brennan sat for his portrait wearing the navy and gold dress uniform, as opposed to the military green uniform which most of the other Chiefs of Staff wore for their portraits, and the result is a most satisfying, realistic portrait. Keating is perhaps best known today for his many intense self-portraits and for his early powerful group portraits of Irish freedom fighters, such as *An IRA Column* of 1921, which forms part of the Hyde Collection at Áras an Uachtaráin. After Maurice MacGonigal, Thomas Ryan was President of the Academy during a number of formative years, when the unfinished Gallagher Gallery in Ely Place was finally improved to a sufficiently suitable state to allow Academy exhibitions to be held there from then onwards. Thomas Ryan was chosen on three occasions to paint portraits for McKee Barracks. His portrait of Lieutenant General Sean McKeown DSM (1973) is at once engaging and sensitively accurate, suggesting a good rapport between the artist and sitter during the studio sessions. He was chosen again in 1989 to paint the portrait of Lieutenant General Tadhg O'Neill DSM and once more in 1998, to paint Lieutenant General Gerry McMahon DSM.

In between times, the McKee Barracks Officers' Mess made some interesting other choices in their selection of artists. It is gratifying to come across the skilful portrait of General Seán Mc Mahon by Margaret Clarke RHA, painted in 1950 at the outset of the collection. She was originally the gifted Margaret Crilly from Newry, who came to study with Orpen at the Metropolitan School of Art where she met and married the brilliant stained-glass artist Harry Clarke RHA, who died all too young of tuberculosis. Margaret Clarke habitually painted still-life and figurative subjects, and the portrait shows how competent she could be when she turned her hand to formal portraiture. Then there is the portrait of Lieutenant General D. Hogan painted by George Collie RHA in 1951. He was a habitual portrait painter, but he also painted many genre subjects in his Schoolhouse Lane studio in Dublin. His work had been somewhat overlooked since his death, until the recent acquisition of a major market scene by the National Gallery of Ireland, who put it on view in the exhibition *Taking Stock Acquisitions 2000-2010* in 2010.

One would expect Seán O'Sullivan RHA to figure prominently among the chosen artists because of his exceptional skill in capturing likenesses in pencil and in oil. He duly shows up with an insightful portrait of Lieutenant General Dan McKenna (1960), which recalls his precocious early talent as exemplified by his many pencil portraits in the collection of the National Gallery of Ireland. They adorned the staircase of the gallery for many years during James White's directorship. O'Sullivan's soulful portrait of Chief of Staff McKenna compares well with his less formal but more passionate, brilliant self-portrait in the National Collection of Artists Self-Portraits at the University of Limerick. That collection now numbers more than 400 works, but they differ from the portraits at McKee Barracks in that they are mostly informal and are in a variety of media and sizes.

Other surprises are Gerald Bruen's portrait of Major General Liam Archer of 1953 and Muriel Brandt's portrait of Major General Liam Egan two years later. Gerald Bruen was primarily a west of Ireland landscape artist but could obviously paint a good portrait when called upon. Belfast-born Muriel Brandt was prone to exaggerate features, including her own, and may have done so in this instance, giving the sitter a squarer jaw line than he actually possessed in reality, it is said. Yet the portrait is strong and decisive, and the sitter must have been satisfied with it. James Le Jeune's 1961 portrait of Major General P.A. Mulcahy is quite a surprise, as the artist is better known as a painter of sunny street scenes teeming with colourfully dressed people. It is not a surprise to discover portraits here by John Coyle RHA, but less well-known names such as Maurice F. Cogan, Richard A. Free, Peter Weafer and Pat Phelan were also commissioned to paint portraits over the years. Maurice F. Cogan was a serving officer in the Engineer Corps of the Army but he practised as an artist throughout his life. He was probably well known and admired by the two Chiefs of Staff who had a say in who was commissioned to paint their official portraits as they reached retirement age. Cogan's portrait of Major General Thomas Leslie O'Carroll also depicts the O'Carroll family crest, as requested by the Chief of Staff. Major General O'Carroll is, unusually, portrayed smiling, unlike most of the other portraits, which are suitably serious. The artist and art teacher Peter Weafer was an F.C.A. officer and was known to his sitter, Lieutenant General Louis Hogan DSM, who asked him to paint his portrait in 1984. The result was very creditable indeed. The portrait of Lieutenant General Carl O'Sullivan DSM was painted by Richard A. Free in 1981. It differs interestingly from most of the other portraits in that it contains a pleasing representation of McKee Barracks itself in the background, where most of the other portraits by the Academy artists have uniform, plain backgrounds.

The last two decades have seen a significant increase in the number of Irish artists specialising in portraiture. Prominent among these have been James Hanley RHA and Conor Walton, a member of the well-known musical family. Hanley won the RDS Taylor Art Prize in his final year at the National College of Art & Design and went on from there to be a prolific representational painter. When he was commissioned to paint the official portrait of Taoiseach Bertie Ahern TD in 2003 by the Office of Public Works, his reputation as a portrait painter was well and truly made, and he has since received numerous commissions. The McKee Barracks Collection holds two portraits by him, and as stated earlier, he is at present engaged in finishing the posthumous portrait of the late Lieutenant General Dermot Earley DSM, which should prove to be a worthy addition to the collection. Hanley likes to have at least two studio sittings of his subject, but is happy to work from good photographs should further sittings not be possible. Conor Walton was also a winner of the RDS Taylor Award for painting and has a very different technique and style from James Hanley. Walton paints in an old master style with infinite attention to detail, ideally requiring many sittings. When he is not painting portraits he paints still-life subjects and allegorical scenes for periodic exhibitions. His portrait of Lieutenant General James Sreenan DSM, painted in 2007, is the most recent commission on view in McKee Barracks, and it holds up very well indeed, being strong and accomplished.

The officers of McKee Barracks have done splendidly since 1950 to assemble such a fine collection of traditional portraits. They must give considerable pleasure to the users of the Mess. They will prove invaluable in the years to come, when historians come to study the pivotal role of the armed forces in the formation and development of the State. Connoisseurs might be forgiven for wondering if the commissioning committees might have been more adventurous in their choice of artists over the years. The same criticism would have to be levelled at the Presidential Portraits and the Portraits of Taoisigh, which have been commissioned from the same reliable pool of academic artists. The only exception to this, perhaps, has been the official portrait of President Mary Robinson painted by Antrim artist Basil Blackshaw HRHA, which hangs in the line in the Áras. Blackshaw is an expressionist experimental painter who occasionally accepts portrait commissions of sitters he admires, and is regarded by some as the best portrait painter in Ireland. His portraits are generally colourful and informal. However, he obviously accepted and adhered to the OPW brief for Áras an Uachtaráin and President Robinson's portrait is a contemporary triumph, without standing out too much from the more formal conventional portraits by Leo Whelan, Seán O'Sullivan, Maurice MacGonigal and others.

A new generation of Irish portrait painters has emerged in recent years, encouraged by an Arnotts National Portrait Award for a period of time, and now succeeded by an annual portrait competition sponsored by Davys, the stock-broking firm. Artists such as Joseph Dunne, Michael O'Dea, James Hanley, immigrant artist Miseon Lee, and many others show portraits in these exhibitions and also at the annual exhibitions of the Royal Hibernian Academy.

Trinity College has favoured artists such as the late Derek Hill CBE, David Hone PPRHA, Andrew Festing, Carol Graham PPRUA, and the late Edward McGuire RHA in recent decades to add to the college collection of portraits. Festing has become a particular Trinity favourite. He was born in Dublin but practises his art in England. The colourful academic gowns give him his opportunity to create dramatic compositions surrounding his sitters, and he usually includes relevant background items to throw more light on the characters and occupations of his subjects. Interestingly, he has not featured in the Áras or Leinster House Collections, nor in the McKee Barracks Collection, which is closest in conception to both of those. He was commissioned, however, to paint a group portrait for the Kildare Street and University Club in St Stephen's Green.

Commissioning portraits costs money and that must have been a regular consideration for the members of the McKee Barracks Officers' Mess, who presumably contributed to the cohesive collection over the last sixty years. They have done well to honour their leaders in this permanent fashion. The portraits will outlive fashion and will constitute a remarkable historic and artistic resource in the years to come.

Dr Patrick J. Murphy HRHA

THE COLLECTION

GENERAL MICHAEL COLLINS

General Michael Collins was born on 16 October 1890 in Woodfield, Sam's Cross, County Cork. He was educated at Lisavaird and Clonakilty national schools. He moved to London in 1905 and joined the British Civil Service. He was sworn into the Irish Republican Brotherhood in 1909 and joined the Irish Volunteers in 1914. General Collins served in the General Post Office during the 1916 Rising and was subsequently interned in Frognoch, Wales. He rose through the ranks of Sinn Féin and the IRA and was both Director of Intelligence and Adjutant General during the War of Independence. General Collins's role during the War of Independence, the Anglo-Irish Truce and the Treaty negotiations was crucial. His organisational abilities – he was also Minister for Finance at the time – and his mastery of counter-intelligence influenced the British authorities to initiate a negotiated settlement. General Collins became Commander-in-Chief of the National Army in 1922 and conducted operations against the Anti-Treaty Forces.

General Collins was killed in action at Béal na mBláth on 22 August 1922.

Leo Whelan RHA

Leo Whelan was born in Dublin on 10 January 1892. He attended the Dublin Metropolitan School of Art and studied under Sir Wiliam Orpen. He first exhibited at the Royal Hibernian Academy (RHA) in 1911 at the age of nineteen, with a portrait of O'Connell Redmond, FRCSI. He was renowned for his portrait painting but did not confine himself to portraiture. Between 1911 and 1956, he contributed each year to the RHA, showing around 250 works in total. He was elected an Associate of the RHA in 1920 and an Academician in 1924. For a number of years, McKee Officers' Mess housed another painting by Leo Whelan, a gift by Dr Risteard Mulcahy. This large-scale work depicts the General Headquarters Staff of the IRA. General Mulcahy, whose portrait by Whelan is also in the collection, was instrumental in having the members of the General Staff sit for the artist. This work now hangs in the National Museum, Collins Barracks. The Mess portrait of General Collins resembles a work submitted by Whelan to the RHA in 1922. He painted portraits of many other prominent subjects, including President William T. Cosgrave, John McCormack, President Douglas Hyde, President Seán T. O'Kelly, President Éamon de Valera and Arthur Griffith. Leo Whelan died on 6 November 1956.

Leo Whelan RHA, 'General M. Collins', 1951. Oil on canvas, 129 x 102 cm.

GENERAL RISTEARD MULCAHY

General Risteard Mulcahy was born on 10 May 1886 in Waterford city. He was educated at the Christian Brothers in Mount Sion, Waterford and in Thurles, and subsequently at University College Dublin. He entered the General Post Office in 1902. In 1907, he joined the Irish Republican Brotherhood, and the Irish Volunteers on their formation on 25 November 1913. He was active during the Easter Rising of 1916 and was Second-in-Command to Thomas Ashe during the Ashbourne action against the Royal Irish Constabulary. He was interned after the Rising, and on his release and return, he became Officer Commander the Dublin Brigade of the Irish Volunteers in 1917. General Mulcahy's sequence of senior military and political appointments is complex. He was Director of Training in the autumn of 1917 and became Chief of Staff in 1918. He was Minister for Defence from January until April 1919 and Assistant Minister for Defence from April 1919 until January 1922. He became Minister for Defence again on 10 January 1922. With General Michael Collins, he conducted operations during the War of Independence. He became Chief of Staff again in July 1922, in addition to Minister for Defence. He became Commander-in-Chief on the death of General Collins on 22 August 1922. General Mulcahy resigned as Minister for Defence and Commander-in-Chief on 19 March 1924.

General Mulcahy died on 16 December 1971.

Leo Whelan RHA

Leo Whelan was born in Dublin on 10 January 1892. He attended the Dublin Metropolitan School of Art and studied under Sir Wiliam Orpen. He first exhibited at the Royal Hibernian Academy (RHA) in 1911 at the age of nineteen, with a portrait of O'Connell Redmond, FRCSI. He was renowned for his portrait painting but did not confine himself to portraiture. Between 1911 and 1956, he contributed each year to the RHA, showing around 250 works in total. He was elected an Associate of the RHA in 1920 and an Academician in 1924. For a number of years, McKee Officers' Mess housed another painting by Leo Whelan, a gift by Dr Risteard Mulcahy. This large-scale work depicts the General Headquarters Staff of the IRA. General Mulcahy, whose portrait by Whelan is also in the collection, was instrumental in having the members of the General Staff sit for the artist. This work now hangs in the National Museum, Collins Barracks. The Mess portrait of General Collins resembles a work submitted by Whelan to the RHA in 1922. He painted portraits of many other prominent subjects, including President William T. Cosgrave, John McCormack, President Douglas Hyde, President Seán T. O'Kelly, President Éamon de Valera and Arthur Griffith. Leo Whelan died on 6 November 1956.

Leo Whelan RHA, 'General R. Mulcahy', 1951. Oil on canvas, 72 x 60 cm.

GENERAL SEAN MCMAHON

General Sean McMahon was born c.1894. He joined the Irish Republican Brotherhood and then the Irish Volunteers at their founding on 25 November 1913. He was active in the Easter Rising as part of the Boland's Mill garrison. He was interned and on his return to Ireland was attached to the Volunteers Headquarters as Quartermaster General. He played an important role as Quartermaster General in supplying warlike stores during the War of Independence. He became Quartermaster General of the Army and then Adjutant General in May 1922. He was appointed as Chief of Staff in August 1922. During his period as Chief of Staff, General McMahon led an official visit to the French Army and laid a wreath at the Tomb of the Unknown Soldier. The government relieved him of his position of Chief of Staff and withdrew his commission on 20 March 1924. However, his commission was reconfirmed on 22 March 1924. General McMahon was appointed as General Officer Commanding Southern Command in October 1925 but resigned due to ill health on 24 January 1927.

General S. McMahon died on 26 March 1955.

Margaret Clarke RHA

Margaret Clarke was born on 29 July 1888 in Newry, County Down. She was awarded a Teachers in Training Scholarship in 1905 to the Dublin Metropolitan School of Art, where she studied under Sir William Orpen. She later taught painting and drawing from life at the school. She married Harry Clarke in October 1914 and after the latter's death in 1931, she undertook the running of his stained-glass studio. She first exhibited at the RHA in 1915 and exhibited more than sixty works in the following forty years. She was elected an Associate of the RHA in 1926 and an Academician in 1927. She was commissioned to paint a series of posters for the Empire Marketing Board in 1930. Her many commissioned portraits include President Éamon de Valera; His Grace, Most Revd John Charles McQuaid, Archbishop of Dublin; and Dr Edward Sheridan, President of the College of Surgeons. She did not, however, confine herself to portraiture, and she won awards for her nude-figure painting. She was active in advancing new approaches to art in Ireland and exhibited with the Dublin Painters in 1938. She helped found the first Irish Living Art Exhibition in 1943 and was on the Executive Committee. Margaret Clarke died on 31 October 1961.

Margaret Clarke RHA, 'General S. McMahon', 1950. Oil on canvas, 74 x 59 cm.

GENERAL EOIN O'DUFFY

General Eoin O'Duffy was born on 20 October 1892 in County Monaghan. Educated locally, he was apprenticed as an engineer in County Wexford and worked as an engineer and architect in his native Monaghan before becoming an auctioneer. General O'Duffy joined the Irish Volunteers in 1917 and was active in the War of Independence, during which he was attached to the Headquarters staff. In March 1921, he commanded the 2 Northern Division. In January 1922, he replaced General Mulcahy as Chief of Staff. General O'Duffy was active during the Civil War and became General Officer Commanding South-Western Command. He resigned from the General Staff on 17 September 1922 to become Commissioner of the Garda Siochána. He returned to the Army on 10 March 1924 and was appointed General Officer Commanding the Forces. His appointment to the role of Inspector General was added to this on 18 March 1924, the day of the Army Mutiny. He ceased to act in these appointments from November 1924.

General O'Duffy died on 13 November 1944.

Seán Keating PPRHA

Seán Keating was born in Limerick on 28 September 1889. In 1911, he won a scholarship to the Dublin Metropolitan School of Art and studied under Sir Wiliam Orpen. He won the Taylor Award in 1914, and a visit to the Aran Islands that year had a lasting influence on his life and on his art. He painted scenes and portraits of participants of the War of Independence. One such work, *Republican Court*, hangs in Collins Barracks, Cork. In 1919, he was appointed as an assistant teacher at the Dublin Metropolitan School of Art and was elected an Associate of the RHA. He was elected an Academician in 1923. He was President of the RHA from 1948 until 1962. In 1937, he was appointed Professor of Painting at the Metropolitan School of Art. He painted a fifty-four-panel mural for Ireland's Pavilion at the New York World Fair in 1939. He completed another government commission for a 3.7 x 7.5 metre mural at the International Labour office in Geneva in 1959. In later life, Keating was considered to be an opponent of modern movements in art. He died on 21 December 1977.

Seán Keating PPRHA, 'General E. O'Duffy', c.1955. Oil on canvas, 75 x 62 cm.

LIEUTENANT GENERAL PEADAR MCMAHON

Lieutenant General Peadar McMahon was born on 10 January 1893 in Ballybay, County Monaghan. He was educated locally and at McGuire's Civil Service College, Dublin. He joined the Irish Volunteers on 25 November 1913. He was active during the Easter Rising, serving in the Stephen's Green garrison and in the College of Surgeons. On his return from internment, he resumed his military activities and was appointed Adjutant of the Limerick Brigade until 1918. He was appointed to the GHQ Staff of the Irish Republican Army in 1919 and held the rank of Commandant in March 1922. He was appointed as General Officer Commanding the Curragh Command in July 1922 and promoted to Major General in January 1923. Lieutenant General McMahon was acting Chief of Staff under General O'Duffy as General Officer Commanding the Forces. He was promoted to Lieutenant General in June 1924 and confirmed in the appointment of Chief of Staff of the Army by the Defence Act of 1924 and by established order of the government on 27 October 1924. Lieutenant General McMahon can thus be considered as the first Chief of Staff of the Defence Forces. He resigned as Chief of Staff on 30 March 1927 and was appointed Secretary of the Department of Defence on 31 March 1927. He continued in this position until 1958.

Lieutenant General McMahon died on 27 February 1975.

Maurice McGonigal PPRHA

Maurice McGonigal, a cousin of the stained-glass artist Harry Clarke, was born in Dublin in 1900. He followed the early career path of some of the subjects of these portraits, by joining the Irish Republican Army and by being interned in Ballykinlar Camp in 1917. His original intention to pursue stained-glass art was changed when he was awarded a Taylor scholarship to the Dublin Metropolitan School of Art in 1923, where he studied under Seán Keating and Patrick Tuohy. He travelled to Holland on a study tour in 1927 and, on his return, he became a visiting teacher to the Royal Hibernian Academy Schools and a substitute teacher at the Metropolitan School of Art. He was elected an Associate of the RHA in 1931 and an Academician in 1933. He became Professor of Painting in 1950 and Keeper to the Academy and was President of the RHA from 1962 until 1977. His first exhibit at the RHA was in 1924 and he continued to exhibit until 1978, averaging five works a year.

Maurice McGonigal was influenced by Seán Keating and painted landscapes and portraits. He had solo exhibitions in the Waddington and Taylor Galleries, and the Hugh Lane Gallery held a retrospective exhibition in 1991. Commissioned to paint a mural for the New York World Fair of 1939, he also painted the interior of Davy Byrne's public house in Dublin. There is a second paining by Maurice McGonigal, *Soldier in Green*, in McKee Officers' Mess. Maurice McGonigal died in 1979.

Maurice McGonigal PPRHA, 'Lieutenant General P. McMahon', 1951. Oil on canvas, 75 x 62 cm.

ACTING LIEUTENANT GENERAL DANIEL HOGAN

Acting Lieutenant General Daniel Hogan was born on 14 July 1895 at Nine Mile House, Carrick-on-Suir, County Tipperary. He was educated locally, joined the railway service and was appointed as a station master's assistant for the Great Northern Railway Company in Clones, County Monaghan. He was active during the War of Independence in the Monaghan area, and was arrested and imprisoned with General O'Duffy. He served as Officer Commanding of the 5 Northern Division from June 1921 until August 1922. He was General Officer Commanding Dublin Command from January 1922 to January 1923 and then General Officer Commanding Eastern Command from that date until March 1927. The Executive Council 'vested the executive military command of the forces in ACTING LIEUTENANT-GENERAL DANIEL HOGAN until further order' on 28 July 1927. Lieutenant General Hogan resigned with effect from 20 February 1929.

Acting Lieutenant General D. Hogan is thought to have died in the United States of America, c.1941.

George Collie RHA

George Collie was born in Carrickmacross, County Monaghan on 14 April 1904. He won the Taylor Scholarship to the Dublin Metropolitan School of Art. He also studied at the Royal College of Art, London and at Paris's Académie de la Grande Chaumière and at Académie Colarossi. On his return to Dublin, he taught at the Dublin Metropolitan School of Art and at his own school in Schoolhouse Lane. Between 1930 and 1975, he exhibited at each RHA exhibition. He was elected an Associate of the RHA in 1933 and an Academician in 1942. He painted many prominent sitters, such as Cardinal Dalton, President de Valera, Taoiseach Liam Cosgrave and Joe Carr. Many of his portraits in the RHA after 1955 were not for sale. He was a member of the Arts Council but resigned for health reasons in 1974. George Collie died on 1 July 1975.

George Collie RHA, 'Acting Lieutenant General D. Hogan', 1951. Oil on canvas, 75 x 62 cm.

LIEUTENANT GENERAL SEAN MCKEON

Lieutenant General Sean McKeon was born in 1893 near Balinalee, County Longford. Educated locally, he went to work with his father, a blacksmith. He joined the Irish Volunteers in 1914 and became Commandant of the 1st Battalion of the Longford Brigade in 1917. He was imprisoned in 1918 and, following his release, he took part in and commanded a number of operations during the War of Independence, the most prominent of which being an ambush of Black and Tans on 3 November 1920. This battle earned him the nickname 'The Blacksmith of Balinalee'. After another successful engagement in 1921, he was captured and sentenced to death, but his release was made a condition of the Anglo-Irish Truce. He was General Officer Commanding Athlone Command in 1923 and was promoted to the rank of Major General on 1 February 1924. He subsequently served as General Officer Commanding the Western Command, General Officer Commanding the Curragh Command, and as Quartermaster General. He was promoted to Lieutenant General and appointed as Chief of Staff on 20 February 1929, following the resignation of Acting Lieutenant General Hogan. He resigned in June 1929, on being nominated as a candidate for TD for Sligo-Leitrim, and he served two terms as Minister for Defence.

Lieutenant General McKeon died on 7 July 1973.

Commandant Maurice F. Cogan

Commandant Maurice F. Cogan was born on 30 January 1913. Initially educated at Synge Street CBS, he was apprenticed as a fitter in Córas Iompair Éireann in 1929, where he moved to the drawing office in 1932. He transferred to the Electricity Supply Board in 1937. He always showed an interest in art and attended night classes at the National College of Art, where he obtained an Art Teacher's Certificate and a silver medal in sculpture. He was close to artistic personalities of the time, in particular Harry Clarke and his wife Margaret. He joined the Corps of Engineer as a private in 1940 and was subsequently commissioned. He served in the Corps of Engineers until he resigned his commission in 1962. He painted throughout this period, exhibiting at the 1937 Exhibition of Irish Art and the RHA in 1939. In addition to his military portrait commissions, he completed many private commissions. He established a printing press in the 1960s. He taught in Dún Laoghaire College and Kevin Street College of Technology. He painted continuously in his later years, moving from portraits to the nude and to expressionist works, with an exhibition in Bray in 2002. M.F. Cogan died on 15 August 2003.

Commandant Maurice F. Cogan, 'Lieutenant General S. McKeon', 1954. Oil on canvas, 75 x 62 cm.

MAJOR GENERAL JOSEPH SWEENEY

Major General Joseph Sweeney was born on 13 June 1897 in Burtonport, County Donegal. He was educated at St Eunan's, Letterkenny and at St Enda's, Rathfarnam under Patrick Pearse. He also studied engineering at University College Dublin. Major General Sweeney joined the Irish Volunteers in 1914 and the Irish Republican Brotherhood in 1915. He fought in the General Post Office during the Easter Rising in 1916. Interned in Frognoch, on his return he resumed his military activities during the War of Independence. He was General Officer Commanding in the north-west during the Civil War and General Officer Commanding Donegal Command from January 1923 until March 1924. Major General Sweeney was acting Chief of Staff for ten days in March 1924 during the events that became known as the 'Army Mutiny'. From 1924 until his appointment as Chief of Staff on 4 June 1929, he occupied most of the General Officer appointments of the Army. He was appointed General Officer Commanding Curragh Command on 31 March 1924, General Officer Commanding Western Command on 18 February 1925, and again General Officer Commanding Curragh Command on 17 June 1927. He was appointed Adjutant General on 15 October 1928 and Quartermaster General on 20 February 1929. His service record is unusual in that on ceasing to be Chief of Staff in October 1931, he continued to serve, first as General Officer Commanding the Curragh Command and then as General Officer Commanding the Western Command, a post to which he was appointed on 29 January 1940. He retired from the Defence Forces with effect from 14 December 1940.

Major General Sweeney died on 20 November 1980.

Commandant Maurice F. Cogan

Commandant Maurice F. Cogan was born on 30 January 1913. Initially educated at Synge Street CBS, he was apprenticed as a fitter in Córas Iompair Éireann in 1929, where he moved to the drawing office in 1932. He transferred to the Electricity Supply Board in 1937. He always showed an interest in art and attended night classes at the National College of Art, where he obtained an Art Teacher's Certificate and a silver medal in sculpture. He was close to artistic personalities of the time, in particular Harry Clarke and his wife Margaret. He joined the Corps of Engineer as a private in 1940 and was subsequently commissioned. He served in the Corps of Engineers until he resigned his commission in 1962. He painted throughout this period, exhibiting at the 1937 Exhibition of Irish Art and the RHA in 1939. In addition to his military portrait commissions, he completed many private commissions. He established a printing press in the 1960s. He taught in Dún Laoghaire College and Kevin Street College of Technology. He painted continuously in his later years, moving from portraits to the nude and to expressionist works, with an exhibition in Bray in 2002. M.F. Cogan died on 15 August 2003.

Commandant Maurice F. Cogan, 'Major General J. Sweeney', 1957. Oil on canvas, 75 x 62 cm.

LIEUTENANT GENERAL
MICHAEL BRENNAN

Lieutenant General Michael Brennan was born on 2 February 1896 in Meelick, County Clare and he was educated at St Munchin's College, Limerick. He joined the Irish Republican Brotherhood in 1911 and the Irish Volunteers in 1913. An active organiser in his native Clare and Limerick, he was imprisoned in 1916 before the Easter Rising. He spent several periods in jail, escaped once, and went on hunger strike on a number of occasions, including the hunger strike which led to the death of Thomas Ashe. Following his release in 1919, he was actively engaged in operations during the War of Independence; he was Commander of the East Clare Brigade in 1918 and Commander of the 1 Western Division in 1921. During the Civil War, Lieutenant General Brennan was in charge of National Army troops in Limerick. He was promoted to the rank of Major General on 24 January 1923, appointed as General Officer Commanding Limerick Command, and then as General Officer Commanding Southern Command on 29 February. He served as Adjutant General between October 1925 and October 1928. In October 1928, he was appointed Inspector General, a position he held until October 1931. He was the only other officer, along with General Eoin O'Duffy, to have held this appointment. On 15 October 1931, he was appointed Chief of Staff, and was three times continued in that appointment, on 16 October 1934, 17 October 1937 and 29 December 1939. He was promoted to the rank of Lieutenant General on 28 January 1940 and retired from the Defence Forces with effect from 29 January 1940.

Lieutenant General Brennan died on 23 October 1986.

Seán Keating PPRHA

Seán Keating was born in Limerick on 28 September 1889. In 1911, he won a scholarship to the Dublin Metropolitan School of Art and studied under Sir Wiliam Orpen. He won the Taylor Award in 1914, and a visit to the Aran Islands that year had a lasting influence on his life and on his art. He painted scenes and portraits of participants of the War of Independence. One such work, *Republican Court*, hangs in Collins Barracks, Cork. In 1919, he was appointed as an assistant teacher at the Dublin Metropolitan School of Art and was elected an Associate of the RHA. He was elected an Academician in 1923. He was President of the RHA from 1948 until 1962. In 1937, he was appointed Professor of Painting at the Metropolitan School of Art. He painted a fifty-four-panel mural for Ireland's Pavilion at the New York World Fair in 1939. He completed another government commission for a 3.7 x 7.5 metre mural at the International Labour office in Geneva in 1959. In later life, Keating was considered to be an opponent of modern movements in art. Seán Keating died on 21 December 1977.

Seán Keating PPRHA, 'Lieutenant General M. Brennan', 1958. Oil on canvas, 75 x 62 cm.

GENERAL DANIEL MCKENNA

General Daniel McKenna was born in Magherafelt, County Derry, on 1 December 1892, and was educated at Rainey Preparatory School, Magherafelt. He joined the Irish Republican Brotherhood in 1913 and the Irish Volunteers in 1915. He joined the South Derry Battalion as a Volunteer and during the War of Independence became successively a Company, Battalion Commander, and by the time of the Anglo-Irish Truce in July 1921, he was Brigade Commander of the 4th Brigade, 2 Northern Division. General McKenna, as Deputy Officer Commanding the 2 Northern Division, was one of those members of the division who moved to the Curragh in September 1922, where he enlisted in the National Army with the rank of Colonel-Commandant and appointed to the Training Staff. In March 1923, he was appointed Adjutant of the Claremorris Command with the rank of Colonel, but returned to the Training Staff at the Curragh in August of the same year. With the reorganisation of the Army in 1924, General McKenna was given the rank of Major and appointed as Adjutant, Southern Command in Cork. He was appointed Deputy Quartermaster General in July 1929. He was promoted to Colonel in July 1931, and was also appointed as a member of the Special Military Tribunal. Between November 1931 and January 1940, General McKenna was successively Director of Supply and Transport, Director of Cavalry, and again Deputy Quartermaster General.

General McKenna's performance in his wide range of appointments brought him to higher attention, and on 29 January 1940, he was promoted directly to the rank of Major General and appointed as Chief of Staff. He held this onerous appointment throughout the period of what was known in Ireland as the 'Emergency', and elsewhere as the Second World War. He was promoted to Lieutenant General on 23 May 1941 and reappointed as Chief of Staff on three occasions. He was promoted to General on 1 December 1948 and retired from the Defence Forces with effect from 30 January 1949.

General McKenna died on 11 April 1975 and, at his own request, his was a civil funeral.

Sean O'Sullivan RHA

Sean O'Sullivan was born in Dublin in 1906. He was awarded a Teacher in Training Scholarship to the Dublin Metropolitan School of Art. He also studied at the Central School of Art in London and at the Académie Julien in Paris, where he was acquainted with James Joyce, Samuel Beckett and Thomas McGreevey. Returning to Dublin, he established himself as a portrait painter and engraver, with a particular interest in lithography. He first exhibited at the RHA in 1926 and continued exhibiting, with an average of six paintings each year, until 1964. He was elected the youngest ever Associate of the RHA in 1928, and an Academician in 1931. During the Emergency, Sean O'Sullivan served in the Naval Service. He painted portraits of many prominent subjects, including Presidents Douglas Hyde and Éamon de Valera, Sir Alfred Chester Beatty, Maude Gonne and Brendan Behan. He did not, however, confine himself to portraiture and painted many landscapes of the West of Ireland. Sean O'Sullivan died of a stroke in 1964.

Sean O'Sullivan RHA, 'General D. McKenna', 1960. Oil on canvas, 75 x 62 cm.

Seán O'Sullivan R.H.A.
1960

LIEUTENANT GENERAL LIAM ARCHER

Lieutenant General Liam Archer was born in Dublin on 18 June 1892 and educated in St Peter's National School. He joined the Irish Volunteers in 1915 and was active during the Easter Rising and the War of Independence. He joined the National Army on 7 March 1922, with the rank of Lieutenant-Commandant. He was promoted to the rank of Colonel on 24 January 1923 and was Director of Signals during the Civil War. The reorganisation of the Army in 1924 saw him granted the rank of Major and his continuance in the appointment of Director of Signals. He was Director of the Volunteer Reserve and the Officer Training Corps in 1929. Promoted to the rank of Colonel on 9 July 1931, he commanded the Dublin Military District. He was Director of Intelligence between 1934 and 1941 and in June 1941 he was appointed as Assistant Chief of Staff, serving as assistant to General McKenna during the Emergency. He continued to serve in this appointment until 1949 and also acted as Officer Commanding the Curragh Command during part of that period. Lieutenant General Archer was promoted to the rank of Major General on 31 January 1949 and succeeded General McKenna as Chief of Staff. He served in this rank until he was promoted to Lieutenant General on 28 January 1952. He retired as Chief of Staff on 30 January 1952.

Lieutenant General Archer died on 22 July 1969.

Gerald Bruen RHA

Gerald Bruen was born in 1908 in Poona, India, where his father, Major William Bruen, was serving with the Connaught Rangers. His father was later decorated with the Military Cross and awarded the OBE. At the age of ten, Gerald's family moved to Dublin. He showed early promise at drawing, painting and draughtsmanship. He enrolled at University College Dublin to study English and History, but did not finish this degree. Instead, he went to attend the Metropolitan School of Art in Dublin, and the Central School of Arts and Crafts in London.

Bruen began exhibiting in 1938, showing watercolours, oils, pastels and lithographs. After the outbreak of the Second World War, he enlisted in the Army and was commissioned. At the Curragh Camp, he came in contact with the republican internees in 'Tintown' and became friends with republican internees Brendan Behan and Máirtín Ó Cadhain. In 1946, he was appointed as an art inspector by the Department of Education, a position which took him around the country. He represented Ireland at many international seminars on art and design. Meanwhile, he continued to paint, returning frequently to the subject of bogland, Dublin Bay, Annamoe, and Laragh in County Wicklow. He was also commissioned to paint several portraits. Elected a full member of the RHA in 1980, he also served as a committee member of both the Arts and Crafts Society and the Watercolour Society of Ireland. His work was shown at several representative Irish exhibitions abroad. He lived in Monkstown, County Dublin for many years, with his wife, Maine Comer. They later moved to Williamstown, County Galway. Gerald Bruen died in 2004.

Gerald Bruen RHA, 'Lieutenant General L. Archer', c.1961. Oil on canvas, 75 x 62 cm.

MAJOR GENERAL LIAM EGAN

Major General Liam Egan was born at Daingean, County Offaly, on 17 December 1895. He was educated at Knockboy College, Carlow and at Maynooth College. He was awarded a Bachelor of Arts Degree from the National University of Ireland in Modern Languages and was a secondary school teacher in Newbridge College, County Kildare. He joined the 3rd Battalion, Offaly No. 1 Brigade in June 1917 and he served as an Intelligence Officer with various units during the War of Independence and the Civil War. He joined the National Army on 29 June 1922 in the rank of Captain and was appointed as Adjutant of the 11th Infantry Battalion in January 1923. Major General Egan was promoted Commandant on 4 September 1923 and served as a General Staff Officer until he was promoted to Major on 9 July 1931. He then served as Assistant Commandant of the Military College as Officer in Charge of the Cadet School. He was promoted to Colonel on 10 October 1940 and appointed as Commandant of the Military College. Later that year, he was appointed Quartermaster General, serving in that appointment throughout the Emergency. In October 1949, Major General Egan was appointed as Officer Commanding the Western Command. He was promoted to the rank of Major General and appointed as Chief of Staff on 31 January 1952. He served as Chief of Staff until 31 December 1954. Major General Egan then reverted to General Officer Commanding Eastern Command until he was reappointed Quartermaster General on 25 April 1958. He retired from that appointment and from the Defence Forces on 17 December 1959.

Major General Egan died on 11 October 1970.

Muriel Brandt RHA

Muriel Brandt was born in Belfast on 19 January 1909. She studied at the Belfast College of Art and at the Royal College of Art, London. She married and lived in Dublin, painting murals, portraits, landscapes and pen-and-ink sketches. One of her finest public works is the panel cycle in the Franciscan church, Merchant's Quay, Dublin. There is also a replica by her of the San Damiano crucifix in the Franciscan Friary, Athlone, in which she has depicted herself, in keeping with medieval artistic practice. Her many portraits include well-known subjects, including a group portrait of Micheál Mac Liammóir, Hilton Edwards and Lady Longford. She was elected an Associate of the Royal College of Art in 1937, and Associate of the RHA in 1948 and an Academician in 1961. She was a member of the Board of the National Gallery of Ireland. Muriel Brandt died on 11 June 1981.

Muriel Brandt RHA, 'Major General L. Egan', c.1961. Oil on canvas, 74 x 60 cm.

LIEUTENANT GENERAL
PATRICK A. MULCAHY

Lieutenant General Patrick A. Mulcahy was born in Waterford City on 4 November 1897, a younger brother of General Risteard Mulcahy. He was educated at Christian Brothers School, Thurles and at St Flannan's College, Ennis. He was employed as a Sorting Clerk and Telegraphist in the General Post Office and then joined the British Army in 1915. Lieutenant General Mulcahy served in the Royal Engineers as a Signaller until 1919. He was posted to France in January 1917 and he was attached to the French 7th Army with a Signals Liaison Unit from September until November 1918. He returned to England, having been recommended for a Cadetship in the Royal Air Force, a position he did not accept, and he was demobilised in January 1919. Lieutenant General Mulcahy joined the Irish Republican Army on 7 March 1919. He served as Assistant Intelligence Officer with the Mid-Clare Brigade and as a Captain with the Tipperary No. 1 Brigade Active Service Unit. In the rank of Colonel Commandant, he served as Officer Commanding Signals of the 3rd Southern Division and of the Curragh Command until June 1922. He was Second in Command and Acting Officer Commanding of the 3rd Southern Command up until January 1923. He was appointed Officer Commanding the Artillery Corps on 29 February 1924 with the rank of Major.

Lieutenant General Mulcahy attended a Field Artillery Staff Course in Larkhill, UK in 1930. He was appointed Director of Artillery on 4 November 1931, an appointment he held until he was appointed Acting and then Officer Commanding the Air Corps on 1 September 1936. He was promoted to the rank of Colonel on 6 April 1939. In 1942, he was reappointed Director of Artillery, a position he held until 2 January 1949, when he was appointed as Officer Commanding Western Command. In October of the same year, he was appointed Quartermaster General. He served on the Chief of Staff's Branch from October 1952 until January 1953, when he was appointed Officer Commanding Eastern Command. He was promoted to Major General on 1 January 1955 and appointed Chief of Staff. He was promoted to Lieutenant General on 31 December 1959 and retired voluntarily from the Defence Forces on 1 January 1960.

Lieutenant General Mulcahy died on 16 May 1987.

James Le Jeune RHA

James George Le Jeune was born in Canada in 1910. His family then moved to Brittany, which is where James was brought up. He went to boarding school in England and studied architecture in London, during which time he continued to paint. He married and moved to Ireland during the 1950s. A noted portrait painter, he was also a seascape and landscape artist and was elected an Academician of the RHA. His works are in many private collections, including in America, and in the National Gallery of Ireland. James Le Jeune died in 1983.

James Le Jeune RHA, 'Lieutenant General P.A. Mulcahy', 1961. Oil on canvas, 72 x 60 cm.

LIEUTENANT GENERAL
SEAN MCKEOWN DSM

Lieutenant General Sean McKeown DSM was born in Castletown, County Louth on 3 June 1910. He entered the Cadet School, the Military College in February 1930 and was commissioned as a Second Lieutenant into the Infantry Corps on 8 September 1931. He was initially posted to the 3rd Infantry Battalion but transferred to the 1st Infantry Battalion on 1 December 1931. He served with the 1st Battalion until 1936 and returned to the 3rd Battalion in 1938. In October 1939, he was appointed Company Commander in the 12th Infantry Battalion and was promoted to Captain on 19 July 1940. His service with the 12th Battalion coincided with the Emergency period. In May 1941, he was appointed Officer Commanding 12th Infantry Battalion and was promoted Acting Commandant on 20 June 1941. He commanded the battalion until 1 March 1946, having been promoted to Lieutenant Colonel on 29 January 1943.

Lieutenant General McKeown was then appointed to the Military College as School Commandant/Cadet Master of the Cadet School. He served in this appointment from 1946 until 1952. He completed a Staff Course at Camberley, UK, in 1947, and was an Instructor in the Infantry School in 1952. He then transferred to Headquarters Western Command as Officer in Charge of Training and Operations Staff. He was appointed Officer Commanding 1st Western Battalion on 5 April 1956 and returned to the Military College in April 1957 as an Instructor in the Command and Staff School. He was promoted to Colonel in December 1957 and appointed Commandant of the Military College. Lieutenant General McKeown was promoted to Major General and appointed Chief of Staff on 1 January 1960. On 1 January 1961, he was appointed as Force Commander of United Nations Forces (ONUC) in the Congo, for which he was awarded the DSM. He was reappointed Chief of Staff with effect from 1 April 1962 upon the cessation of his appointment with the United Nations. He was again reappointed Chief of Staff for a period of five years from 1 April 1966. He retired from the Defence Forces on 1 April 1971.

Lieutenant General McKeown died on 30 July 1998.

Thomas Ryan PPRHA

Thomas Ryan was born in Limerick in 1929 and educated in the Christian Brothers School, Limerick, the School of Art, Limerick, and the National College of Art & Design, Dublin under Seán Keating and Maurice MacGonigal. He is married to Mary Joyce and has four sons and two daughters. He is an established artist whose work hangs in major collections and he was the designer of the one pound coin and Millennium fifty pence.

Among his many achievements, he was President of the Royal Hibernian Academy of Arts from 1982 to 1992 and Chairman of the RHA Trust; Honorary Member of the Royal Academy, London and Royal Scottish Academy, Edinburgh; Governor of the National Gallery of Ireland, 1979-82; President of the United Arts Club, Dublin; President of the Limerick Art Society; Associate of the National College of Art & Design; Council Member of the Watercolour Society of Ireland; Board Member of the Stamp Design Committee for An Post; Founder Member of the European Council of National Academies of Fine Art (Madrid); Member of Council 'The British School at Rome'; Council Member of 'The British Institution', London, 1983-93; Knight of the Order of St Lazarus of Jerusalem; Knight Commander of the Equestrian Order of the Holy Sepulchre of Jerusalem; Member of the Order of Dom Carlos Primera of Portugal, and Doctor of Letters from the University of Limerick.

Thomas Ryan PPRHA, 'Lieutenant General S. McKeown', 1973. Oil on canvas, 75 x 65 cm.

LIEUTENANT GENERAL
SEAN COLLINS-POWELL

Lieutenant General Sean Collins-Powell was born in Clontarf, Dublin on 12 January 1905. He joined the Irish Volunteers in January 1920 and served during the War of Independence with the 1st Cork Brigade and with the Cork City Column. He joined the National Army as a Second Lieutenant in 1922. His initial service was with the 10th and 15th Battalions, and in 1926 he was posted to Defence Plans Division, Army Headquarters. In September 1926, he attended an Infantry Officers' Course at Fort Benning, USA. He also completed a two-month study tour, including a course in light and heavy tanks in Fort Meade in 1927. This experience led to his transfer in 1928 to the Armoured Car Corps, forerunner of the Cavalry Corps. He was promoted to Captain on 1 September 1931 and served in various appointments in the Armoured Car Corps until, after promotion to the rank of Commandant in April 1939, he was appointed as Acting Commandant of the Military College on 18 November 1940.

Lieutenant General Collins-Powell was promoted to the rank of Acting Colonel on 24 July 1942 and was appointed as Officer in Charge of Plans and Operations in Army Headquarters in January 1943. He served in this Emergency appointment until he was appointed Officer Commanding the Curragh Command in November 1944, where he served until he was appointed Officer Commanding Western Command in October 1951. He returned to the Southern Command as Officer Commanding in January 1955, until his appointment as Quartermaster General in December 1959. Lieutenant General Collins-Powell was promoted to the rank of Major General on 1 January 1961 and appointed Chief of Staff during Lieutenant General McKeown's service in the Congo. He served as Chief of Staff until 1 April 1962 and was appointed Adjutant General on 18 April 1962. He retired from the Defence Forces with effect from 12 January 1969.

Lieutenant General Collins-Powell died on 13 October 1991.

Commandant Maurice F. Cogan

Commandant Maurice F. Cogan was born on 30 January 1913. Initially educated at Synge Street CBS, he was apprenticed as a fitter in Córas Iompair Éireann in 1929, where he moved to the drawing office in 1932. He transferred to the Electricity Supply Board in 1937. He always showed an interest in art and attended night classes at the National College of Art, where he obtained an Art Teacher's Certificate and a silver medal in sculpture. He was close to artistic personalities of the time, in particular Harry Clarke and his wife Margaret. He joined the Corps of Engineers as a private in 1940 and was subsequently commissioned. He served in the Corps of Engineers until he resigned his commission in 1962. He painted throughout this period, exhibiting at the 1937 Exhibition of Irish Art and the RHA in 1939. In addition to his military portrait commissions, he completed many private commissions. He established a printing press in the 1960s. He taught in Dún Laoghaire College and Kevin Street College of Technology. He painted continuously in his later years, moving from portraits to the nude and to expressionist works, with an exhibition in Bray in 2002. M.F. Cogan died on 15 August 2003.

Commandant Maurice F. Cogan, 'Lieutenant General S. Collins-Powell', 1973. Oil on canvas, 100 x 75 cm.

MAJOR GENERAL PATRICK DELANEY

Major General Patrick Delaney was born on 30 April 1916 in Toomevara, County Tipperary and was educated at Christian Brothers School, Nenagh. He entered the Volunteer Force on 30 August 1934, and the Cadet School, the Military College, as a private on 21 January 1935. He was commissioned as a Second Lieutenant to the Infantry Corps and posted to the 3rd Infantry Battalion on 7 September 1939. He commanded a company in the 3rd Battalion with the rank of Acting Lieutenant in August 1941. He served as a Staff Officer on the Plans and Operations Staff of Army Headquarters with the rank of Acting Captain in 1942 and 1943, before being appointed as Second in Command of the 8th Infantry Battalion in November 1943. Major General Delaney was promoted to Commandant on 18 August 1944 and was Second in Command of the 3rd Infantry Battalion in 1947, before returning to Army Headquarters as a Staff Officer.

Major General Delaney completed a Company Commander's Course at the School of Infantry, Warminster, UK in 1947. He was appointed as an Instructor in 1949, and then as Chief Instructor of the Command and Staff School with the rank of Lieutenant Colonel in October 1959. He continued as Chief Instructor, when not serving overseas, until he was appointed as a Staff Officer in the Plans and Operations Branch at Army Headquarters in December 1965. Promoted Colonel on 12 June 1968, he was appointed Commandant of the Military College. Major General Delaney was appointed as Director of Intelligence on 9 April 1970. He was promoted to the rank of Major General on 1 April 1971 and appointed Chief of Staff. He served with the United Nations Force in the Congo (ONUC) as Officer Commanding the 38th Infantry Battalion from October 1962 until May 1963. He commanded the 42nd Infantry Battalion UNFICYP in Cyprus between March and October 1965.

Major General Delaney died in service on the 27 July 1971.

Richard A. (Dick) Free

Richard Free is a somewhat elusive figure. He was a pupil of George Collie and presented his work in an exhibition of paintings and drawings by George Collie's student group in April 1952, and in a Sunday Painters' exhibition in 1956. In his earlier years, he practised the technique of scraper-board drawing and was praised for the imagination of his work. He was a portrait painter and figure draughtsman. He ran George Collie's studio in Schoolhouse Lane for some time after Collie's death in 1975. He subsequently became an art teacher, advertising life classes in Dublin in the 1980s.

Richard A. Free, 'Major General P. Delaney', 1983. Oil on canvas, 75 x 62 cm.

MAJOR GENERAL THOMAS L. O'CARROLL

Major General Thomas Leslie O'Carroll was born in Clontarf, Dublin on 19 December 1917. He was educated at Colaiste Muire and entered the Cadet School, the Military College on 28 October 1937. He was commissioned as a Second Lieutenant in the Infantry Corps on 7 September 1939 and posted to the 4th Infantry Battalion in Cork. He was appointed as Adjutant of the 4th Battalion, and on promotion to Acting Captain, appointed as Assistant Operations Officer of the 1st Division on 11 August 1941. He was appointed Company Commander in the 21st Infantry Battalion in February 1943 and promoted to Commandant in November 1943. He continued to serve in the Southern Command in the 7th Brigade Headquarters and as Officer Commanding the Command Training Depot until December 1947, when he was appointed as Adjutant of the Curragh Training Camp. He was posted as a Staff officer in the Adjutant General's Branch in January 1948 and served as Aide to An tUachtarán from October 1949 until October 1953.

He then returned to the Adjutant General's Branch before being posted as Personal Staff Officer to the Chief of Staff. He was promoted to Lieutenant Colonel on 16 January 1958 and appointed Officer in Charge of Administration Section, Adjutant General's Branch. Major General O'Carroll was Executive Officer of the Eastern Command from May 1960 until January 1961, with the rank of Acting Colonel. He was appointed Deputy Quartermaster General in January 1961, promoted to Colonel on 13 March 1961, and served in that appointment until February 1968. He was appointed Commandant of the Military College from February 1968 until 29 July 1971. On 30 July 1971 he was promoted to the rank of Major General and appointed as Chief of Staff. He retired from the Defence Forces on 29 July 1976.

Major General O'Carroll died on 11 March 1981.

Commandant Maurice F. Cogan

Commandant Maurice F. Cogan was born on 30 January 1913. Initially educated at Synge Street CBS, he was apprenticed as a fitter in Córas Iompair Éireann in 1929, where he moved to the drawing office in 1932. He transferred to the Electricity Supply Board in 1937. He always showed an interest in art and attended night classes at the National College of Art, where he obtained an Art Teacher's Certificate and a silver medal in sculpture. He was close to artistic personalities of the time, in particular Harry Clarke and his wife Margaret. He joined the Corps of Engineer as a private in 1940 and was subsequently commissioned. He served in the Corps of Engineers until he resigned his commission in 1962. He painted throughout this period, exhibiting at the 1937 Exhibition of Irish Art and the RHA in 1939. In addition to his military portrait commissions, he completed many private commissions. He established a printing press in the 1960s. He taught in Dún Laoghaire College and Kevin Street College of Technology. He painted continuously in his later years, moving from portraits to the nude and to expressionist works, with an exhibition in Bray in 2002. M.F. Cogan died on 15 August 2003.

Commandant Maurice F. Cogan, 'Major General T.L. O'Carroll', 1983. Oil on canvas, 75 x 62 cm.

LIEUTENANT GENERAL
CARL O'SULLIVAN DSM

Lieutenant General Carl O'Sullivan was born on 18 October 1919 and educated at Tralee Christian Brothers Schools. He entered the Cadet School, the Military College on 27 September 1938 and was commissioned as a Second Lieutenant into the Infantry Corps on 23 October 1939. He was posted to the 9th Infantry Battalion as a Platoon Commander and was appointed as Second in Command of the Battalion in May 1943. He was promoted to Lieutenant in September 1941, to Captain in March 1942 and to Commandant in November 1943. He was appointed as a Company Commander in the 13th Infantry Battalion in 1946 and as Second in Command of the 6th Infantry Battalion in February 1947. Lieutenant General O'Sullivan completed a Company Commander's Course at the School of Infantry, Warminster, UK and was posted to the Infantry School in November 1947.

In 1957, he was appointed as Camp Commandant of the Internment Camp in the Curragh. He was appointed to the 13th Infantry Battalion as Commanding Officer on his promotion to Lieutenant Colonel on 16 January 1958. Lieutenant General O'Sullivan returned to the Curragh as Executive Officer in March 1959. He was promoted to Colonel and appointed Officer Commanding the 4th Brigade on 5 October 1959. A period of service in the Military College saw him as Commandant of the Command and Staff School from March 1961 and then Commandant, the Military College from September 1962 until February 1968. He was appointed Officer Commanding the Southern Command in February 1968, a position he held until being appointed Quartermaster General on 8 March 1971. The appointment of Adjutant General followed in September 1975, and on 29 July 1976 he was promoted to Major General and appointed Chief of Staff. He was promoted to Lieutenant General on 16 August 1978. Lieutenant General O'Sullivan served as Assistant Chief of Staff at headquarters UNFICYP in Cyprus from October 1964 until April 1965.

Lieutenant General O'Sullivan retired from the Defence Forces with effect from 2 June 1981. Lieutenant General O'Sullivan died on 10 September 2008.

Richard A. (Dick) Free

Richard Free is a somewhat elusive figure. He was a pupil of George Collie and presented his work in an exhibition of paintings and drawings by George Collie's student group in April 1952, and in a Sunday Painters' exhibition in 1956. In his earlier years, he practised the technique of scraper-board drawing and was praised for the imagination of his work. He was a portrait painter and figure draughtsman. He ran George Collie's studio in Schoolhouse Lane for some time after Collie's death in 1975. He subsequently became an art teacher, advertising life classes in Dublin in the 1980s.

Richard A. Free, 'Lieutenant General C. O'Sullivan DSM', 1982. Oil on canvas, 90 x 74 cm.

LIEUTENANT GENERAL LOUIS HOGAN DSM

Lieutenant General Louis Hogan was born on 4 April 1921 in Newmarket-on-Fergus, County Clare and entered the Cadet School, the Military College in November 1940. He was commissioned into the Infantry Corps in October 1941 with the rank of Temporary Second Lieutenant. He served in the 8th Infantry Battalion (Thomond) as a Platoon Commander and Mortar Officer until December 1944, by which time he had been promoted to the rank of Lieutenant. Lieutenant General Hogan served as a Staff Officer in G1 Branch in Army Headquarters between 1944 and 1946, before returning to his early speciality as Mortar Platoon Commander with both the 3rd Infantry and 5th Infantry Battalions. He served as a Staff Officer in Training Section, Chief of Staff's Branch, Army Headquarters, as both a Captain and a Commandant between 1958 and 1971. He served as Second in Command of the 5th Infantry Battalion and Officer Commanding the 7th Infantry Battalion (FCA) in 1971 and 1973. Lieutenant General Hogan was promoted to Acting Lieutenant Colonel in 1973 and appointed as Officer Commanding of the newly formed 27th Infantry Battalion. He was successively Operations Officer and Executive Officer of the Eastern Command from 1976 to 1978. He was promoted to Acting Colonel in 1978 and appointed Director of Intelligence, Chief of Staff's Branch, and promoted to Colonel in January 1980. March 1980 saw him promoted to the rank of Brigadier General and appointed as General Officer Commanding, Western Command. He was promoted to Major General in December 1980 and appointed as Quartermaster General. He was appointed as Chief of Staff on his promotion to Lieutenant General on 2 June 1981.

Lieutenant General Hogan served with the United Nations Observer Group in Lebanon (UNOGIL) between August and December 1958. He was a Company Commander with the 33rd Infantry Battalion (ONUC) in the Congo in 1960-1. He served with the 4th Infantry Group (UNFICYP) in Cyprus in 1965 and as a Military Observer with UNTSO in the Middle East between 1969 and 1971.

Lieutenant General Hogan retired as Chief of Staff on 4 April 1984. He died on 21 June 2001.

Commandant Peter Weafer ANCA

Born in Dublin in 1929, Peter Weafer graduated from the School of Design at the National College of Art in 1954. He started his career working as a graphic artist in London before returning to Ireland to take up a position with *The Kerryman* in Tralee. His teaching career began at the Technical School, Ballinasloe, County Galway, before he moved to Templeogue College CSSP Dublin, where he worked for twenty-five years. Weafer works in oils, watercolours and pastels, executing portraits, landscapes, etc. He served under General Louis Hogan when he was Battalion Commander of the 7th Infantry Battalion, FCA. The posthumous portrait of Commandant T. Wickham which hangs in the Military College was painted at the request of General Hogan. He was subsequently commissioned to do the General's portrait as Chief of Staff. Another of Weafer's works of military interest is the posthumous portrait of Lieutenant O'Curry, which hangs in Mullingar Barracks. Much of his work is in private collections in England, the US, Canada and Ireland.

Commandant Peter Weafer ANCA, 'Lieutenant General L. Hogan DSM', 1984. Oil on canvas, 75 x 60 cm.

LIEUTENANT GENERAL
GERALD O'SULLIVAN DSM

Lieutenant General Gerald O'Sullivan was born on 10 February 1923 in Dublin, and entered the Cadet School, the Military College on 20 November 1941. He was commissioned into the Infantry Corps on 25 May 1943 as a Second Lieutenant in the 14th Infantry Battalion. He served as a Training Officer in the Eastern Command Training Depot between 1946 and 1958, before being appointed as a Staff Officer at Defence Forces Headquarters. He held appointments in Intelligence Section, Plans and Operations Section and Operations Section, Chief of Staff's Branch, in the ranks of Captain and Commandant between 1958 and 1974. He was promoted Lieutenant Colonel and commanded the 2nd Infantry Battalion between November 1976 and July 1978, when he was appointed Executive Officer at Headquarters 3rd Brigade. He was promoted to Colonel in December 1980 and served as Executive Officer Eastern Command, Deputy Adjutant General, Officer Commanding Eastern Command FCA and Director of Plans and Research, before being promoted to the rank of Brigadier General in March 1981 and appointed as General Officer Commanding, Eastern Brigade. Lieutenant General O'Sullivan was promoted to Major General in January 1984, and then to Lieutenant General in April 1984, when he was appointed Chief of Staff.

Lieutenant General O'Sullivan served at Headquarters ONUC in the Congo in 1961-2. He was Intelligence Officer of the 4th Infantry Group (UNFICYP) in Cyprus. He served in Headquarters UNFICYP between October 1970 and October 1971, and again between August 1974 and July 1976. Lieutenant General O'Sullivan was awarded a Distinguished Service Medal for his service in Cyprus as Chief Economics Officer at UNFICYP HQ during the invasion by Turkish Forces. He also acted as Military Advisor to Lieutenant General Prem Chand during Anglo-American talks for the independence of Zimbabwe in 1977, and during talks for the independence of Namibia in 1980.

Lieutenant General O'Sullivan retired as Chief of Staff on 10 February 1986. Lieutenant General G. O'Sullivan died on 21 June 2010.

John Coyle RHA

John Coyle is a graduate of the National College of Art, Dublin. He has worked in Spain, France and Italy and is well known as a portrait and still-life painter. His work is in many private collections, as well as in the National Self-Portrait Collection, Dáil Éireann and College of Physicians. He has been a tutor in Dún Laoghaire College of Art, Head of the Art Department in Blackrock College and tutor in the National College of Art & Design, Dublin. He is presently Professor of Painting in the Royal Hibernian Academy and he lives and works in Dublin.

John Coyle RHA, 'Lieutenant General G. O'Sullivan DSM', 1986. Oil on canvas, 86 x 69 cm.

LIEUTENANT GENERAL TADHG O'NEILL DSM

Lieutenant General Tadhg O'Neill was born on 16 October 1926 in Castlecomer, County Kilkenny, and educated at Christian Brothers Schools, Carlow. He entered the Cadet School, the Military College on 3 December 1946 and was commissioned as a Second Lieutenant into the Artillery Corps on 11 November 1948. He served in a series of regimental appointments between then and January 1967, including Troop Commander, Instructor Officer and Battery Commander in the Depot Artillery, the 2nd Field Artillery Regiment and the 1st Anti-Aircraft Regiment. He was promoted to Lieutenant in November 1950, Captain in December 1957 and Commandant on 8 June 1971. He was posted to Plans and Operations Section, Chief of Staff's Branch on the 13 January 1967. He held the appointments of Officer in Charge of A and Q Matters in this branch between 1967 and July 1978. He was then appointed Camp Commandant McKee Barracks and Officer Commanding McKee Barracks Company, and promoted to the rank of Acting Lieutenant Colonel. Lieutenant General O'Neill was appointed School Commandant, the Artillery School in October 1978, Officer Commanding the 2nd Field Artillery Regiment on 2 March 1979 and promoted to Lieutenant Colonel on 13 June 1979. He was promoted to Colonel on 2 March 1982 and appointed as Executive Officer Western Command in September 1983. On 26 February 1984, he was promoted to the rank of Brigadier General and appointed General Officer Commanding the Western Command. He was promoted to Major General on 9 February 1986, to Lieutenant General on 10 February 1986 and appointed Chief of Staff the same day.

He served with Headquarters ONUC in the Congo from February 1961 to March 1962. He was Staff Officer with Headquarters UNFICYP from January 1968 until July 1968. Between April 1981 and January 1982, he served as Senior Operations Officer UNIFIL in the Lebanon, and between January 1982 and May 1983, he was Military Assistant to the Force Commander UNIFIL.

Lieutenant General O'Neill retired from the Defence Forces with effect from 16 October 1989. He died on 17 September 2009.

Thomas Ryan PPRHA

Thomas Ryan was born in Limerick in 1929 and educated in the Christian Brothers School, Limerick, the School of Art, Limerick, and the National College of Art & Design, Dublin under Seán Keating and Maurice MacGonigal. He is married to Mary Joyce and has four sons and two daughters. He is an established artist whose work hangs in major collections and he was the designer of the one pound coin and Millennium fifty pence.

Among his many achievements, he was President of the Royal Hibernian Academy of Arts from 1982 to 1992 and Chairman of the RHA Trust; Honorary Member of the Royal Academy, London and Royal Scottish Academy, Edinburgh; Governor of the National Gallery of Ireland, 1979-82; President of the United Arts Club, Dublin; President of the Limerick Art Society; Associate of the National College of Art & Design; Council Member of the Watercolour Society of Ireland; Board Member of the Stamp Design Committee for An Post; Founder Member of the European Council of National Academies of Fine Art (Madrid); Member of Council 'The British School at Rome'; Council Member of 'The British Institution', London, 1983-93; Knight of the Order of St Lazarus of Jerusalem; Knight Commander of the Equestrian Order of the Holy Sepulchre of Jerusalem; Member of the Order of Dom Carlos Primera of Portugal, and Doctor of Letters from the University of Limerick.

Thomas Ryan PPRHA, 'Lieutenant General T. O'Neill DSM', 1989. Oil on canvas, 99 x 84 cm.

LIEUTENANT GENERAL JAMES PARKER DSM

Lieutenant General James Parker was born in Mitchelstown, County Cork, on 15 April 1929. He entered the Cadet School, the Military College in May 1948 and was commissioned in the rank of Second Lieutenant to the Infantry Corps in May 1950. His served in the General Training Depot until 1952, when he was transferred to the Southern Command. He served with the 4th Infantry Battalion and as Assistant Command Adjutant until he was posted to the Military College in October 1959, on his promotion to Captain. Lieutenant General Parker served as an instructor in the Cadet School, Infantry School and the Command and Staff School. He completed a Company Commander's course in Warminster, UK in 1959 and a Staff course at Camberley, UK in 1963. Lieutenant General Parker received his Bachelor of Arts from University College Dublin in 1973. In 1975, he served as a Staff Officer in Operations Section, Chief of Staff's Branch, at Defence Forces Headquarters. He was appointed Officer Commanding 3rd Infantry Battalion in March 1979 and promoted to Lieutenant Colonel in 1980. Lieutenant General Parker returned to the Curragh Command in 1980 as Officer in Charge of Operations Section. He was promoted to Acting Colonel in 1982 and appointed as Director of Reserve Forces, before becoming Officer Commanding 2nd Brigade in 1983. He was Executive Officer of both the Western and Curragh Commands between 1985 and 1987, before being promoted to Brigadier General in 1988 and to Major General in March 1989, when he was appointed as Adjutant General of the Defence Forces. He was promoted to Lieutenant General and appointed as Chief of Staff on 16 October 1989.

Lieutenant General Parker first served overseas as Platoon Commander, Intelligence Platoon and Assistant Intelligence Officer of the 35th Infantry Battalion (ONUC) in the Congo in 1961. He was Operations Officer of the 9th Infantry Group (UNFICYP) in Cyprus in 1967-8. He was Officer Commanding the 26th Infantry Group (UNEF) in the Middle East in 1974 and served as a Military Observer (UNTSO) between 1977 and 1979, also in the Middle East. He served at Headquarters UNIFIL in the Lebanon as Staff Officer Special Projects in 1984-5. Lieutenant General Parker served two tours of duty as Chief Military Observer with the United Nations Military Observer Group India and Pakistan (UNMOPGIP) between 1987 and 1989.

Lieutenant General Parker retired on 15 April 1992 and resides in County Kildare.

Pat Phelan ANCA

Pat Phelan was born in Portlaw, County Waterford in 1937. He studied at the Waterford Art School under Robert Bourke and then at the National College of Art. Professor Julius and Seán Keating were among his teachers at the college. A triple portrait by him of Seán Keating was exhibited at the RHA in 1975. A noted portrait painter, he has completed hundreds of commissions. He worked in advertising and design before deciding to become a full-time artist in 1971, establishing a studio in Dublin's Dawson Street. He has painted many Taoisigh and prominent politicians, most notably a portrait of President de Valera which hangs in the office of An Taoiseach. He has been commissioned to portray, among many other personalities, the chairmen and directors of RTÉ and the deans of UCD's Faculty of Medicine. He has held many exhibitions in Dublin and in his native Waterford. While no longer active professionally, Pat Phelan continues to paint members of his family. He resides in Terenure, Dublin.

Pat Phelan ANCA, 'Lieutenant General J. Parker DSM', 1992. Oil on canvas, 97 x 75 cm.

LIEUTENANT GENERAL
NOEL BERGIN DSM

Lieutenant General Noel Bergin was born on 25 December 1931 at Cherrymills, Kildangan, County Kildare. He entered the Cadet School, the Military College in November 1950 and was commissioned into the Artillery Corps in November 1952 in the rank of Second Lieutenant. Following early service in various artillery appointments, including the Artillery School, he was posted as an instructor to the Cadet School, the Military College with the rank of Captain in December 1961. He completed the 34th Staff Course, Camberley, in 1963, and in 1971, on promotion to the rank of Commandant, he was posted as an instructor to the Command and Staff School, the Military College. He was subsequently posted to Operations Section, Chief of Staff's Branch at Defence Forces Headquarters and to the 2nd Field Artillery Regiment, before promotion to the rank of Lieutenant Colonel in 1980. As Lieutenant Colonel, he filled the appointments of Cadet School Commandant and Officer Commanding the Army Apprentice School. In 1984, he was promoted to Colonel and served as Military Advisor, Irish Delegation, Conference on Confidence and Security Building Measures and Disarmament in Stockholm, Sweden. Lieutenant General Bergin took his Bachelor of Arts Degree at University College Dublin in Politics, Economics and History. He subsequently served as Officer Commanding, Eastern Command Infantry Force, from 1985 until being appointed Director of Operations at Defence Forces Headquarters in 1987. He was promoted twice in 1990, to Brigadier General and then to Major General, with the appointment of Adjutant General to the Defence Forces in June 1990. He was promoted to the rank of Lieutenant General and appointed Chief of Staff on 15 April 1992.

Lieutenant General Bergin served as Platoon Commander, Intelligence Platoon, and as Assistant Intelligence Officer in the 34th Infantry Battalion (ONUC) in the Congo in 1961, and as Assistant Information Officer in the 40th Infantry Battalion (UNFICYP) in Cyprus in 1964. He was Second in Command of the 44th Infantry Battalion (UNIFIL) in Lebanon in 1978-9.

Lieutenant General Bergin retired from the Defence Forces on 8 February 1995 and resides in County Kildare.

John Coyle RHA

John Coyle is a graduate of the National College of Art, Dublin. He has worked in Spain, France and Italy and is well known as a portrait and still-life painter. His work is in many private collections, as well as in the National Self-Portrait Collection, Dáil Éireann and College of Physicians. He has been a tutor in Dún Laoghaire College of Art, Head of the Art Department in Blackrock College and tutor in the National College of Art & Design, Dublin. He is presently Professor of Painting in the Royal Hibernian Academy and he lives and works in Dublin.

John Coyle RHA, 'Lieutenant General N. Bergin DSM', 1995. Oil on canvas, 86 x 68 cm.

LIEUTENANT GENERAL GERARD MCMAHON DSM

Lieutenant General Gerard McMahon was born in Limerick City on 22 August 1935 and was educated at Sexton Street Christian Brothers Schools. He entered the Cadet School, the Military College in 1953 and was commissioned into the Infantry Corps in November 1955 in the rank of Second Lieutenant. His first posting was to the 6th Infantry Battalion in Athlone. Between commissioning and 1969, he spent most of his service in various units of the Western Command. In January 1970, on completion of a Staff Course in Camberley, UK, he was posted to the Military College as an instructor. In 1975 he was awarded a Bachelor of Arts Degree in Economics and History from University College Dublin. Between 1970 and 1978, he served in the Cadet School, the Infantry School and the Command and Staff School of that college. Subsequently, he served as Executive Officer of the General Training Depot before moving to Operations Section, Chief of Staff's Branch at Defence Forces Headquarters in Dublin. In the mid-1980s, he commanded the 5th Infantry Battalion in Collins Barracks, Dublin. On promotion to Colonel in 1991, he was appointed Director of Planning and Research in the Chief of Staff's Branch. On promotion to Brigadier General in 1992, he was appointed Commandant, the Military College, and in March 1993 he was promoted to Major General and appointed Quartermaster General of the Defence Forces. He was appointed Chief of Staff with the rank of Lieutenant General on 8 February 1995.

Lieutenant General McMahon's United Nations service began when he served as a Platoon Commander with the 37th Infantry Battalion (ONUC) in the Congo in 1962. In 1971-2 he served as Operations Officer of the 21st Infantry Group (UNIFCYP) in Cyprus. In 1978-9 he was Operations Officer of the 44th Infantry Battalion (UNIFIL) in Lebanon and in 1987-8 he was Senior Operations Officer at UNIFIL Headquarters. He spent two years with UNTSO in the Middle East as an Observer, between 1982 and 1984. In 1990, he served at UN Headquarters in New York.

Lieutenant General McMahon retired from the Defence Forces on 22 August 1998 and resides in County Kildare.

Thomas Ryan PPRHA

Thomas Ryan was born in Limerick in 1929 and educated in the Christian Brothers School, Limerick, the School of Art, Limerick, and the National College of Art & Design, Dublin under Seán Keating and Maurice MacGonigal. He is married to Mary Joyce and has four sons and two daughters. He is an established artist whose work hangs in major collections and he was the designer of the one pound coin and Millennium fifty pence.

Among his many achievements, he was President of the Royal Hibernian Academy of Arts from 1982 to 1992 and Chairman of the RHA Trust; Honorary Member of the Royal Academy, London and Royal Scottish Academy, Edinburgh; Governor of the National Gallery of Ireland, 1979-82; President of the United Arts Club, Dublin; President of the Limerick Art Society; Associate of the National College of Art & Design; Council Member of the Watercolour Society of Ireland; Board Member of the Stamp Design Committee for An Post; Founder Member of the European Council of National Academies of Fine Art (Madrid); Member of Council 'The British School at Rome'; Council Member of 'The British Institution', London, 1983-93; Knight of the Order of St Lazarus of Jerusalem; Knight Commander of the Equestrian Order of the Holy Sepulchre of Jerusalem; Member of the Order of Dom Carlos Primera of Portugal, and Doctor of Letters from the University of Limerick.

Thomas Ryan PPRHA, 'Lieutenant General G. McMahon DSM', 1998. Oil on canvas, 100 x 85 cm.

LIEUTENANT GENERAL DAVID STAPLETON DSM

Lieutenant General David Stapleton was born on 25 September 1937 in Clonmel, County Tipperary. He entered the Cadet School, the Military College on 1 December 1955 and was commissioned as a Second Lieutenant into the Supply and Transport Corps on 25 November 1957. Between his date of commissioning and January 1967, he occupied appointments in the 1st Field Supply and Transport Company and the Supply and Transport Depot, as Platoon Commander and as Military Analyst and Instructor. He was promoted to Captain on 13 January 1967 and appointed as a Staff Officer in the Directorate of Supply and Transport. He returned to the Supply and Transport Depot in the same month and continued to serve there as an Instructor and Administration Officer until he was promoted to Commandant in March 1976. He was then appointed as Adjutant of the 6th Brigade. Lieutenant General Stapleton completed a Staff Course in Camberley, UK, in 1977. Following the Staff Course, he was appointed as an Instructor in the Military College in March 1978. He returned to the Supply and Transport Depot in November 1983 and was appointed as Officer Commanding Vehicle Workshops in January 1986. Lieutenant General Stapleton was promoted to the rank of Lieutenant Colonel in September 1988 and was appointed as Officer in Charge of Operations Planning Sub-section in Operations Section, Chief of Staff's Branch. He was promoted to Colonel on 2 September 1991 and appointed Officer Commanding 6th Brigade. He was promoted to Brigadier General on 26 January 1995 and to Major General on 8 February 1995, when he was appointed as Quartermaster General. He was promoted to Lieutenant General and appointed Chief of Staff on 22 August 1998.

Lieutenant General Stapleton first overseas service was as a Transport Platoon Officer with the 37th Infantry Battalion (ONUC) in the Congo from May to November 1962. He was a Military Observer with UNTSO in the Middle East from October 1972 until April 1974. He served twice with UNIFIL in the Lebanon, as Second Command of the 53rd Infantry Battalion, from March to November 1983, and as Transport Group Commander of the 57th Infantry Battalion. He served with the United Nations Transition Assistance Group (UNTAG) in Namibia from March 1989 until March 1990. On 1 June 1997, he was appointed Force Commander of the United Nations Disengagement Observer Force (UNDOF) on the Syrian Golan Heights, where he served until he was appointed Chief of Staff.

Lieutenant General Stapleton retired from the Defence Forces with effect from 25 September 2000 and resides in County Kildare.

James Hanley RHA

James Hanley is a Dublin-based painter. An established portrait artist, painting many official and State portraits, he is represented in significant public, corporate and private collections in Ireland and abroad. Born in 1965, he graduated from University College Dublin in 1987 with a degree in History of Art and English, and from the National College of Art & Design in 1991 with a BA in Fine Art (Painting). He works in a representational style, in both painting and drawing. He has exhibited extensively in group exhibitions in Ireland and abroad, and has had seven solo exhibitions. James is a full Member of the Royal Hibernian Academy; he was elected to Aosdána in 2008 and recently elected to the Board of Governors of the National Gallery of Ireland.

James Hanley RHA, 'Lieutenant General D. Stapleton DSM', 2007. Oil on canvas, 120 x 90 cm.

LIEUTENANT GENERAL COLM MANGAN DSM

Lieutenant General Colm Mangan was born in Dublin on 21 February 1941. He was educated at Rockwell College, County Tipperary, and entered the Cadet School, the Military College on 25 January 1960. He was commissioned as a Second Lieutenant into the Infantry Corps, and posted to the General Training Depot in the Curragh on 11 December 1961. He served as a Platoon Commander in the Army Apprentice School between May 1963 and September 1968. He was promoted to Captain and appointed as a Company Commander in the 3rd Infantry Battalion in October 1968. He returned to the Army Apprentice School as Adjutant and Company Commander in June 1969. Between 1974 and 1979, he served as Deputy Governor of the Military Detention Barracks, Adjutant 3rd Infantry Battalion and Company Commander in the 30th Infantry Battalion. Lieutenant General Mangan was promoted to Commandant in July 1977 and appointed as a Staff Officer in Operations Staff of the Curragh Command. He completed a Staff Course in Germany – the Generalstabslehrgang at Führungsakademie der Bundeswehr – in 1977, and was then appointed as an Instructor in the Command and Staff School at the Military College. In 1985, he was appointed as a Staff Officer in Operations Section, Chief of Staff's Branch. Promoted to Lieutenant Colonel in June 1989, he was appointed as Officer Commanding the 3rd Infantry Battalion and then as Officer in Charge of Planning Sub-section in Operations Section, Chief of Staff's Branch. Lieutenant General Mangan was promoted to Colonel on 24 May 1993 and appointed as Director of Military Police and Provost Marshall. He was promoted to Brigadier General and appointed Commandant of the Military College in March 1995, and then as General Officer Commanding the Eastern Command in May 1996. Promoted to Major General on 29 November 1998 and appointed Deputy Chief of Staff (Support), he was promoted to Lieutenant General on 25 September 2000 and appointed as Chief of Staff.

Lieutenant General Mangan served as a Platoon Commander with the 3rd Infantry Group (UNFICYP) in Cyprus from July 1964 until January 1965. He served with UNFICYP again as Assistant Adjutant of the 10th Infantry Group in 1968. He was a Military Observer with UNTSO in the Middle East from December 1972 until August 1974 and he served twice with UNIFIL in the Lebanon, as Operations Officer with the 57th Infantry Battalion in 1985 and as Officer Commanding the 68th Infantry Battalion in 1990-1. He served as a Monitor with the CSCE Mission in Yugoslavia in 1991-2.

Lieutenant General Mangan retired from the Defence Forces with effect from 21 February 2004 and resides in County Kildare.

James Hanley RHA

James Hanley is a Dublin-based painter. An established portrait artist, painting many official and State portraits, he is represented in significant public, corporate and private collections in Ireland and abroad. Born in 1965, he graduated from University College Dublin in 1987 with a degree in History of Art and English, and from the National College of Art & Design in 1991 with a BA in Fine Art (Painting). He works in a representational style, in both painting and drawing. He has exhibited extensively in group exhibitions in Ireland and abroad, and has had seven solo exhibitions. James is a full Member of the Royal Hibernian Academy; he was elected to Aosdána in 2008 and recently elected to the Board of Governors of the National Gallery of Ireland.

James Hanley RHA, 'Lieutenant General C. Mangan DSM', 2003. Oil on canvas, 120 x 90 cm.

LIEUTENANT GENERAL
JAMES SREENAN DSM

Lieutenant General James Sreenan was born in Ballymote, County Sligo on 28 June 1944, and was educated at Coláiste Muire, Ballymote. He entered the Cadet School, the Military College, in October 1962 and was commissioned into the Infantry Corps in September 1964 in the rank of Second Lieutenant. His first appointment was as a Platoon Commander in the 5th Infantry Battalion. From commissioning until 1973, he spent most of his service in the Eastern Command, holding appointments in the 5th Infantry Battalion, at Command Headquarters, and in the 20th Infantry Battalion (FCA), where he was appointed as Training Officer of a newly established Irish-speaking company. Following a staff course in Camberley, UK, in 1973, he was posted to the Military College as an Instructor in the Infantry School and later the Cadet School, where he was Chief Instructor. Lieutenant General Sreenan holds a Bachelor of Arts Degree in History and Politics from University College Dublin and a Diploma in Adult and Community Education from NUI Maynooth. In 1984, he returned briefly to the 5th Infantry Battalion and was posted that same year as a Staff Officer to Training Section, Chief of Staff's Branch at Defence Forces Headquarters. He later served as a Staff Officer in Planning and Research Section, as a Commandant and as Lieutenant Colonel. On promotion to Colonel in 1996, he was appointed Deputy Quartermaster General. He was promoted to Brigadier General in 1999, and in September 2000 he was promoted to Major General and appointed to the position of Deputy Chief of Staff (Support). He was promoted to Lieutenant General and appointed Chief of Staff on 21 February 2004.

Lieutenant General Sreenan's United Nations service began when he served as a Platoon Commander in the 9th Infantry Group (UNFIYCP) in Cyprus in 1967. From 1975 to 1977, he served as a Military Observer with UNTSO in the Middle East. He was Company Commander, A Company of the 57th Infantry Battalion (UNIFIL) in Lebanon in 1985, and from 1989 to 1991 he served a Staff Officer at the Headquarters of UNFICYP. In 1994-5 he commanded the 76th Infantry Battalion (UNIFIL) in Lebanon. From May 1999 to August 2000, he served as Deputy Force Commander UNIFIL.

Lieutenant General Sreenan retired on 28 June 2007 and resides in County Kildare.

Conor Walton RHA

Conor Walton was born in Dublin in 1970 and studied in the National College of Art & Design, Dublin, from which he graduated in 1993 with a Joint Honours Degree in the History of Art and Fine Art (Painting). He received a special commendation and prize for his thesis, 'Abstraction: A Discourse on Language and Painting'. After reading for an MA in Art History and Theory at the University of Essex, which he was awarded with distinction in 1995, he spent some time in Florence, studying painting and old master techniques with Charles Cecil. He returned to Dublin in 1996, and had his first solo exhibition there in 1998. Conor now lives and works near Ashford, County Wicklow. His sixth solo exhibition, 'Sacred and Profane', took place in England at Beaux Arts, Bath in September 2010. He has received many awards and also a scholarship from The Elizabeth Greenshields Foundation, Canada, which enabled him to study in Italy. Conor's works are held in many public collections in Ireland and his commissioned portraits can be found in public and private collections throughout the country. His work has featured on book covers and postage stamps in Ireland and abroad.

Conor Walton RHA, 'Lieutenant General J. Sreenan DSM', 2007. Oil on linen, 120 x 80 cm.

LIEUTENANT GENERAL DERMOT EARLEY DSM

Lieutenant General Dermot Earley was born on 24 February 1948. He was educated at St Nathy's College, Ballaghadereen, County Roscommon, and joined the Defence Forces as a Cadet in 1965. He was commissioned into the Infantry Corps in 1967 and appointed as a Platoon Commander in the Recruit Training Depot in the Curragh. He specialised in Physical Training and Education, and was appointed an Instructor at the Army School of Physical Culture (ASPC) in 1969. He held a variety of operational and administrative appointments in the Curragh Command, and completed the First Ranger Course in the Defence Forces in 1969. He also completed a specialist Diploma Course, with distinction, in physical education at St Mary's College, Strawberry Hill, Twickenham, in 1970-1. He graduated from the Royal College of Defence Studies London (2001) and held a Master of Arts (Hons) in Peace and Development Studies from the University of Limerick (1999).

Following a period as Assistant Command Adjutant at Curragh Command Headquarters, Lieutenant General Earley was appointed School Commandant of the ASPC. From 1983 to 1987, he was Desk Officer for Overseas Operations, and later Current Operations, in the Chief of Staff's Branch at Defence Forces Headquarters. On return from an overseas posting in 1991, he was appointed an instructor at the Command and Staff School of the Military College, and in 1994-5 he helped establish the United Nations Training School Ireland (UNTSI) in the college.

On promotion to Lieutenant Colonel in 1995, he commanded the 27th Infantry Battalion on the border with Northern Ireland and held further appointments as OIC Conciliation and Arbitration, and OIC Public Relations at Defence Forces Headquarters. He was promoted to Colonel in 2001 and held the appointments of Director of Administration and Director of Personnel, before being selected for promotion to Brigadier General in December 2003. Lieutenant General Earley was promoted to Major General in February 2004 and was appointed Deputy Chief of Staff (Support). He was appointed Chief of Staff of the Defence Forces on 28 June 2007.

Lieutenant General Earley served with UNTSO in the Middle East from 1975 to 1977. He was Adjutant of the 52nd Infantry Battalion with UNIFIL (Lebanon) in 1982-3. He served as the Deputy Military Advisor to the Secretary General of the United Nations at UN Headquarters in New York from 1987 to 1991 and he commanded the 81st Infantry Battalion with UNIFIL in 1997.

Lieutenant General Earley resigned from the Defence Forces on 9 June 2010 and died on 23 June 2010.

James Hanley RHA

James Hanley is a Dublin-based painter. An established portrait artist, painting many official and State portraits, he is represented in significant public, corporate and private collections in Ireland and abroad. Born in 1965, he graduated from University College Dublin in 1987 with a degree in History of Art and English, and from the National College of Art & Design in 1991 with a BA in Fine Art (Painting). He works in a representational style, in both painting and drawing. He has exhibited extensively in group exhibitions in Ireland and abroad, and has had seven solo exhibitions. James is a full Member of the Royal Hibernian Academy; he was elected to Aosdána in 2008 and recently elected to the Board of Governors of the National Gallery of Ireland.

James Hanley RHA, 'Lieutenant General D. Earley DSM', 2010. Oil on canvas, 120 x 90 cm.

NOTES

1   It is important to make clear that General Michael Collins was not Chief of Staff but Commander-in-Chief. Richard Mulcahy was his Chief of Staff up to Collins's death in August 1922. On the death of Collins, Mulcahy became Commander-in-Chief, with Sean McMahon being his Chief of Staff. I am indebted to Commandant Billy Campbell for enlightening me on this important issue.

2   Defence Forces Regulations A13, paragraph 9.

3   Minute Book, Officers' Mess, McKee Barracks. This essay is based on the proceedings of General Mess Meetings, Mess Committee Meetings and the Mess President's Files. A debt of gratitude is owed to the Officer Commanding the Mess, and most particularly to the Mess President, Commandant Pauline O'Connell, who has been untiring in her co-operation and assistance in providing access to these invaluable sources. Subsequent quotations, other than from Defence Forces Regulations, are from these documents.

4   Defence Forces Regulations A13.

5   Bodkin, Thomas, 'Problems of National Portraiture', *The Burlington Magazine for Connoisseurs*, Vol.69, No.405, December 1936 (The Burlington: London), p.251.

6   Quoted in Soussloff, Catherine M., *The Subject in Art: Portraiture and the Birth of the Modern* (Duke University Press: Durham & London, 2006), p.37.

7   Bodkin, Thomas, 'Problems of National Portraiture', *The Burlington Magazine for Connoisseurs*, Vol.69, No.405, December 1936 (The Burlington: London), pp246-51. See also Cullen (2004), pp55-60, for a more lengthy discussion on this subject.

8   Brilliant, Richard, *Portraiture* (Reaktion Books: London, 1997), p.7.

9   Flynn, James, Letter to Professor J. Keating, 18 December 1958, Mess President's Files, McKee Officers' Mess.

10   West, Shearer, *Portraiture* (Oxford University Press: Oxford, 2004), p.59.

11   Campbell, Lorne, 'Portraiture', *Grove Art Online*, *Oxford Art Online*, 21 December 2010.

12   Brilliant, Richard, *Portraiture* (Reaktion Books: London, 1997), p.23.

13   Bodkin, Thomas, 'Problems of National Portraiture', *The Burlington Magazine for Connoisseurs*, Vol.69, No.405, December 1936 (The Burlington: London), p.246.

14   MacNally, Niamh, *Catching a Likeness: Portraits on Paper* (National Gallery of Ireland: Dublin, 2007), p.2.

15   West, Shearer, *Portraiture* (Oxford University Press: Oxford, 2004), p.43.

16   Cullen, Fintan, *The Irish Face: Redefining the Irish Portrait* (National Portrait Gallery Publications: London, 2004), p.60.

17   Cullen, Fintan, *The Irish Face: Redefining the Irish Portrait* (National Portrait Gallery Publications: London, 2004), p.18.

18   West, Shearer, *Portraiture* (Oxford University Press: Oxford, 2004), p.71.

19   The late Colonel Dan Bryan, who in 1924 was an intelligence officer in Eastern Command, quoted in Eunan O'Halpin, *Defending Ireland: The Irish State and its Enemies Since 1922* (Oxford, 1999), p.50.

20   Department of Defence, *The White Paper on Defence: Review of Implementation* (Dublin, 2007).

21   O'Malley, Michael, *Military Aviation in Ireland, 1921-45* (UCD Press: Dublin, 2010), pp241-70.

22   Horner, David, *The Australian Centenary History of Defence Volume IV: Making the Australian Defence Force* (Melbourne, 2001), p.40. There is clear evidence of an aspiration for an integrated three-arm defence force in the thoughtful document submitted by the Representative Association of Commissioned Officers (RACO) in 1999, during the drafting of the *White Paper on Defence* eventually published in February 2000.

23   Farrell, Brian, *Chairman or Chief? The Role of the Taoiseach in Irish Government* (Dublin, 1971).

24   GHQ records for 1921 and 1922 are in the Mulcahy Papers (P7A, B, and C) in the University College Dublin Archives; Thomas Brennan Papers (private collection).

25   Committee of Public Accounts, *Report on Appropriation Accounts, 1926-7* (Dublin, 1928), pp133-5.

26   O'Neill, T.P. and the Earl of Longford, *Éamon de Valera* (Dublin, 1970), p.335.

27   Author's interview with Colonel Dan Bryan, 1983. The late Lieutenant Colonel Sean Clancy also remarked on McKenna's ferocious tongue (Author's interview, 1997).

28   O'Halpin, *Defending Ireland*, p.258.